Law Enforcement Tools:
Techniques for Reliability Assessment

Wayne L. Davis, Ph.D.

Law Enforcement Tools: Techniques for Reliability Assessment

Wayne L. Davis, Ph.D.

Copyright © 2017 by Wayne L. Davis, Ph.d.

| ISBN: | Softcover | 978-1-5434-6426-9 |
| | eBook | 978-1-5434-6427-6 |

Any people depicted in stock imagery provided by Thinkstock are models, and such images are being used for illustrative purposes only.
Certain stock imagery © Thinkstock.

Print information available on the last page.

Rev. date: 11/16/2017

To order additional copies of this book, contact:
Xlibris
1-888-795-4274
www.Xlibris.com
Orders@Xlibris.com
768769

Illustrators

Dawn Larder

Ariana Greer

Derrick Freeman

Editor

Sheri Browning, Ph.D.

Preface

This book has been written to assist criminal justice college students who are interested in conducting academic research on hardware (police tools). First, this book describes Weibull analysis and its usefulness. Second, this book provides an example for assessing the reliability of products by testing them to failure. Indeed, it is quite important to be able to predict when law enforcement tools will fail in the field, especially if only a very small sample size is available for data analysis. Finally, this book explains how to use normal probability plots to enhance reliability and to reduce the number of scrap parts created during the manufacturing process. This can be described graphically by manipulating the average size and variance of the machined pieces during a production run.

Table of Contents

List of Tables

List of Figures

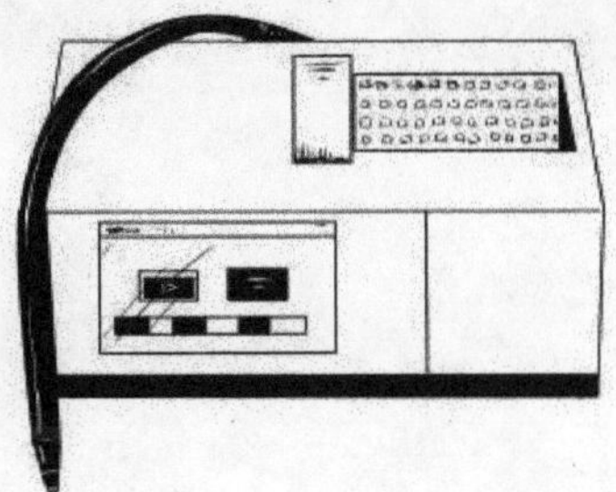

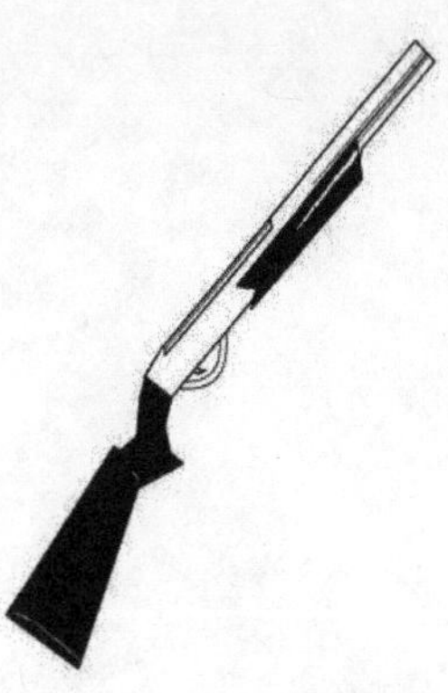

CHAPTER 1

Reliability Testing: Test-to-Failure Analysis

Figure 1. Time to failure. How long will police equipment survive in the field?

Law Enforcement Equipment

All police officers must think of their jobs in terms of meeting the public's needs and expectations. Police officers must strive for continuous improvements by preventing problems and by identifying improvement opportunities. An important issue for police departments is to have functional tools and to solve any equipment problems before the officers have a chance to experience them in the field.

Police officers use a number of tools (i.e., hardware) in various environments, many of which may be harsh. Therefore, the tools need to be tested-to-failure in the various environments in which they will be used. Some of the variables that may cause tools to fail may include vibration, humidity, salt, dirt, pressure, metal fatigue,

wear, and temperature. Reliability information on the

survivability of the tools need to be determined.

Figure 2. A police radio in a very cold environment.

It is important that law enforcement tools and equipment be durable because lives may depend upon them. Sometimes, police departments may need to modify standard tools and equipment, such as the electrical system in a police car, in order to add a specific radio system. In other cases, officers may need to use a typical police tool in a new environment or there may be exigent circumstances in which an officer may need to push a tool to its limit. In short, there may be a lack of reliability data on the police tools in those particular situations and environments.

If police departments know that these situations may occur, and there is a lack of data, then the department should obtain reliability data on the tools in those situations. In addition, even if tools have been tested-to-failure in specific environments, it is important to understand the test results. Making decisions on information that is not well understood is risky and dangerous.

It is important to be able to predict when police tools and equipment will fail so that they can be replaced when necessary (or not purchased in the first place). The Weibull distribution statistical analysis can be used to predict the failure characteristics of a population based on a very small sample size (King, 1971). This technique is very useful because, when a new tool is being developed and decisions are being made about whether or not to invest in the product, there may only be a few expensive

prototypes available.

Weibull Distribution Analysis

In 1951, Wallodi Weibull proposed the use of a

mathematical function that could be applied to various

survivor curves (Grant & Leavenworth, 1980; King,

1971). This mathematical function, called the Weibull

distribution, was popularized for its use in electronic

failure analysis. The Weibull distribution is a continuous

distribution and is applicable for sample sizes fewer than

30 (King, 1971). It is highly desirable to have a minimum

sample size of 7 failed units (versus suspended items),

and an absolute minimum sample size of 5 failed units.

The Weibull Distribution is applicable in describing a

wide variety of patterns of variation, including departures from the normal and exponential. The Weibull plot is particularly useful for learning about a system's reliability and provides information about the nature of a failure and its distribution (McLinn, 1986).

The Weibull probability paper has a log scale on the horizontal axis and a log-log scale on the y-axis (Chatfield, 1983; Ford Motor Company, 1968; King, 1971). This is important because, as will be discussed in Chapter 2, it allows the data to be plotted in the following format: $y = mx + b$. The x-axis represents the measured data values (e.g., hours to failure) and the y-axis represents the accumulated percent values (i.e., median rank values).

An assumption of Weibull distribution is that the data are independently identically distributed (Marshall, 2012). In addition, if it is not possible to draw a straight line through the points plotted on Weibull probability paper, then either the minimum life parameter is not zero (this problem may be managed by transforming the data) or the failures are not Weibull distributed (Catalano, 1973). If the failures are not Weibull distributed, then Weibull probability paper cannot be used. If a straight line can be plotted, then any deviation from the straight line can be considered sampling error (Kapur & Lamberson, 1977).

The Weibull probability density function has three parameters that provide valuable information. Estimates of the parameters are obtained directly from the straight-line plot. The three parameters are described below

(Catalano, 1973; Dodson, 2006; Grant & Leavenworth,

1980; Kapur & Lamberson, 1977; Marshall, 2012;

Weibull.com, 2002, April). See Figures 3-6.

Shape parameter, β, is the slope parameter, which

indicates the failure rate.

Scale parameter, η , is the characteristic life

parameter. The characteristic life is the number

of hours at which 63.2% of all failures will have

occurred.

Location parameter, ɣ, is the failure free life or

minimum life parameter.

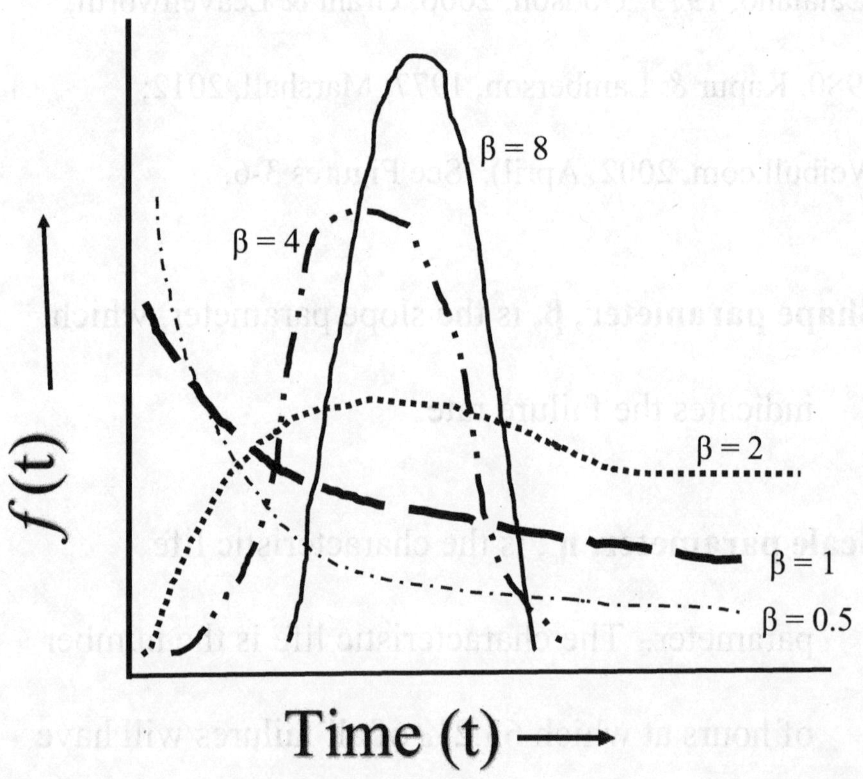

Figure 3. Weibull shape (slope) parameter, β, on **graph paper** (Weibull.com, 2002, April). The effect of the Weibull shape parameter on the probability density function (the value of ɣ is constant).

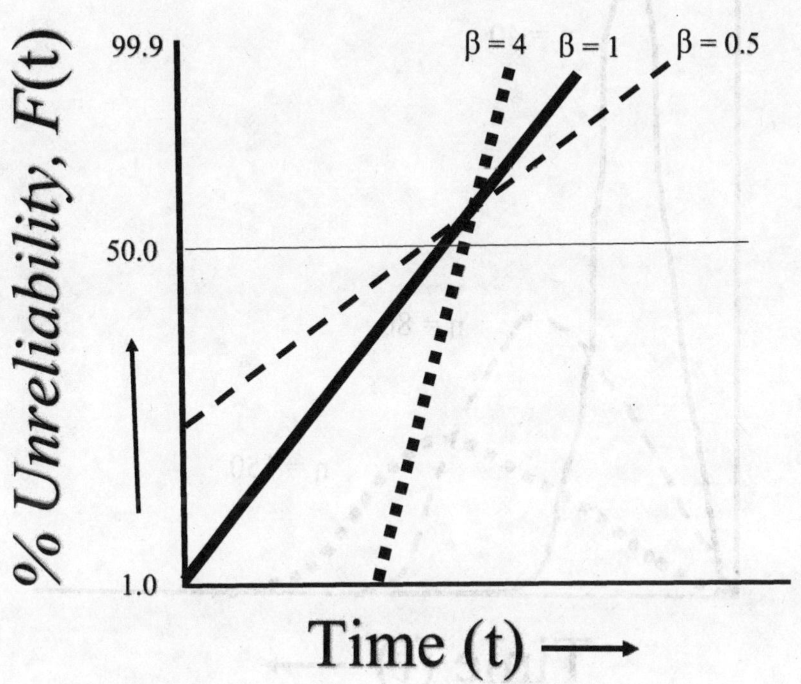

Figure 4. The effect of the Weibull slope (shape) parameter, β, on **Weibull probability plot paper** (the value of η is constant) (Weibull.com, 2002, April).

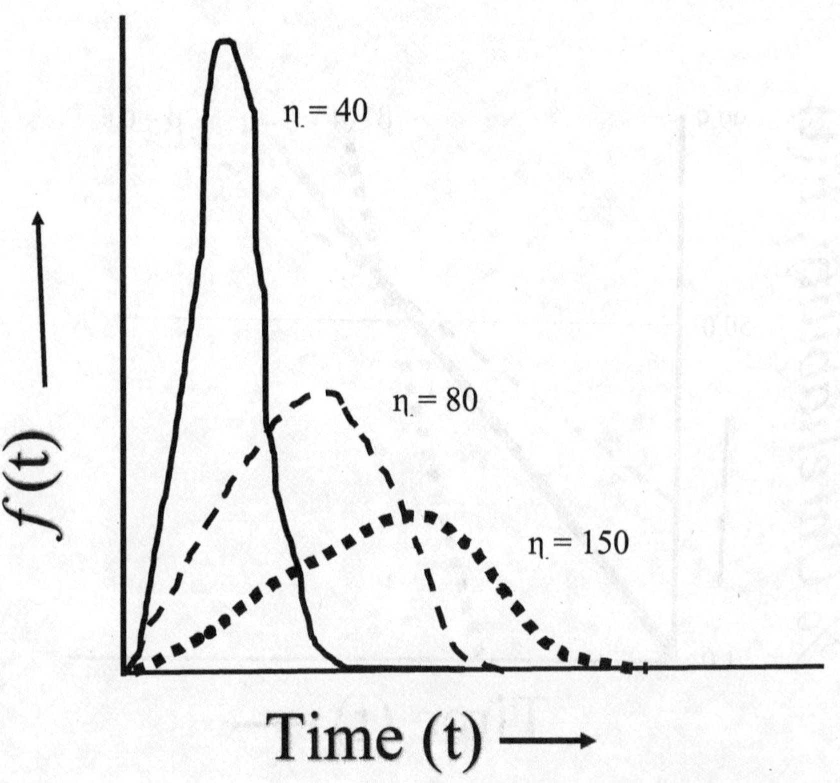

Figure 5. Weibull scale (characteristic life) parameter, η, on **graph paper**. The effect of the scale parameter on the probability density function (the value of β is constant) (Weibull.com, 2002, April).

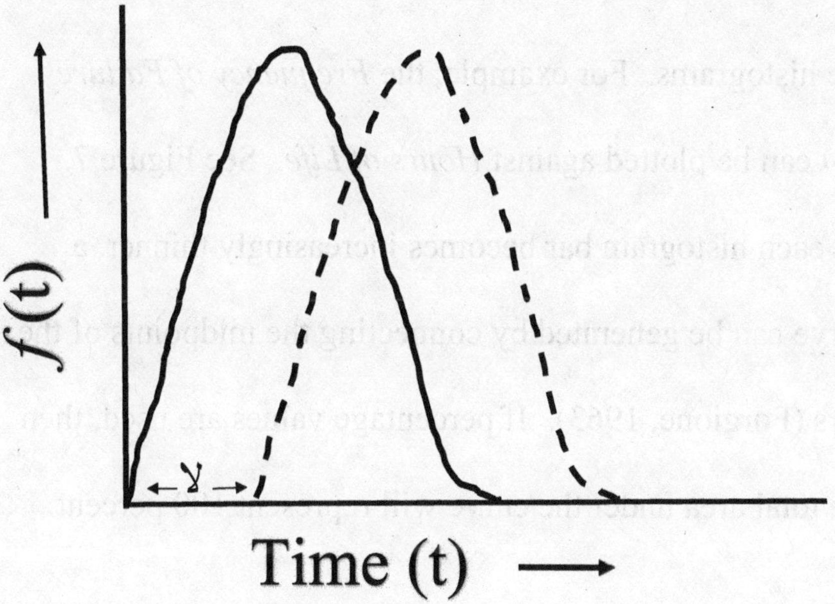

Figure 6. The Weibull location (minimum life) parameter, Ɣ, on **graph paper**. The effect of the location parameter on the probability density function. The location parameter indicates the earliest time-to-failure of the items being tested. When Ɣ = 0, the distribution starts at time = 0 (Weibull.com, 2002, May).

Distribution of Failures

One way to describe the distribution of failures is to use histograms. For example, the *Frequency of Failure (%)* can be plotted against *Hours of Life*. See Figure 7. As each histogram bar becomes increasingly thinner, a curve can be generated by connecting the midpoints of the bars (Forgione, 1963). If percentage values are used, then the total area under the curve will represent 100 percent.

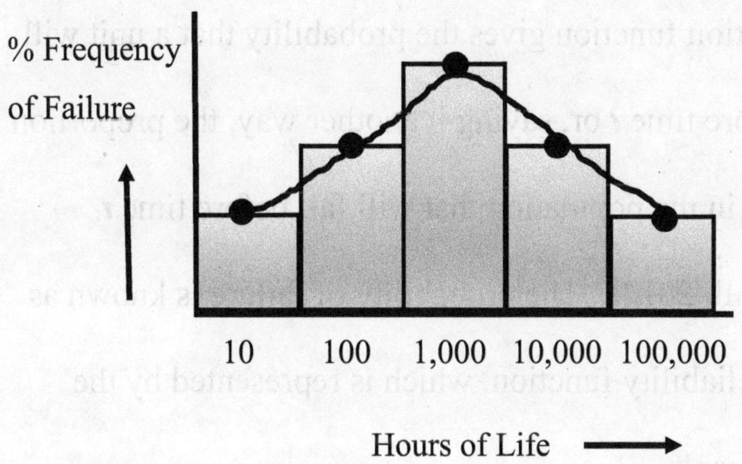

Figure 7. Using a histogram to describe the distribution of failures over time (semi-logarithmic plot).

A more useful way to represent the failure rate is to

present the cumulative failure rate, $f(t)$, up to a specific

point in time, t (Forgione, 1963). The cumulative

distribution function gives the probability that a unit will

fail before time t or, saying it another way, the proportion

of units in the population that will fail before time t.

(Marshall, 2012). The probability of failure is known as

the unreliability function, which is represented by the

median rank.

When comprehensive information on the failure

history of the population is unavailable, the true rank of

each failure in the population is unknown (Ford Motor

Company, 1969). In order to make a statistical estimate

of each failed item's rank, a sample can be used to

determine an estimate in which the positive and negative errors effectively cancel each other out (in the long run). This estimate is called the median rank.

A median rank is the estimated value that the true probability of failure should have at a specific ordered failure in the sample during the test-to-failure analysis at a 50% confidence level (Dodson, 2006; Weibull, 2001, October). The median rank is a nonparametric estimate of the cumulative distribution function based on ordered failures. Thus, the data on all failed units in the sample need to be arranged in ascending order. In short, the median rank represents the cumulative percent failed that is to be assigned to each item in the sample.

By utilizing median ranks, the percentage of units in the population that will fail before time *t* can be estimated (Forgione, 1963; Marshall, 2012). The percent failed is the area under the curve from zero to the time in question. If the curve generated in Figure 7 is plotted as the cumulative distribution of failures, then the plot will assume an S shape (See Figure 8). The number of failures (represented by the height of the bars in Figure 7) is smallest at 10 and 100,000 hours. Consequently, the change in the frequency of failures will be smallest at 10 hours and 100,000 hours. According to Figure 7, most of the failures occur at 1,000 hours. Thus, there is a greater change in the frequency of failures at this time (i.e., greater slope). The cumulative failure rate is a very good model that can be used to describe the life characteristics

of various law enforcement tools.

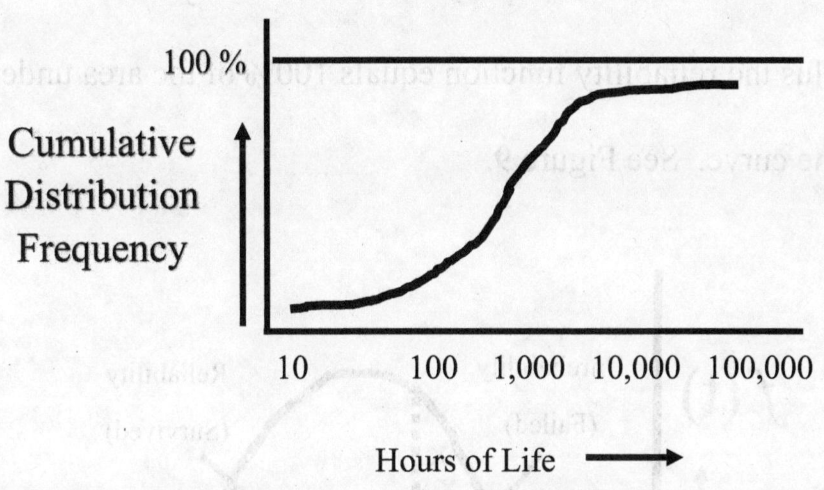

Figure 8. The cumulative failure rate (semi-logarithmic plot).

The probability of success is known as the reliability function while the probability of failure is known as the unreliability function (Lyer, 2013; Marshall, 2012; Weibull.com, 2002, April). The unreliability function plus the reliability function equals 100% of the area under the curve. See Figure 9.

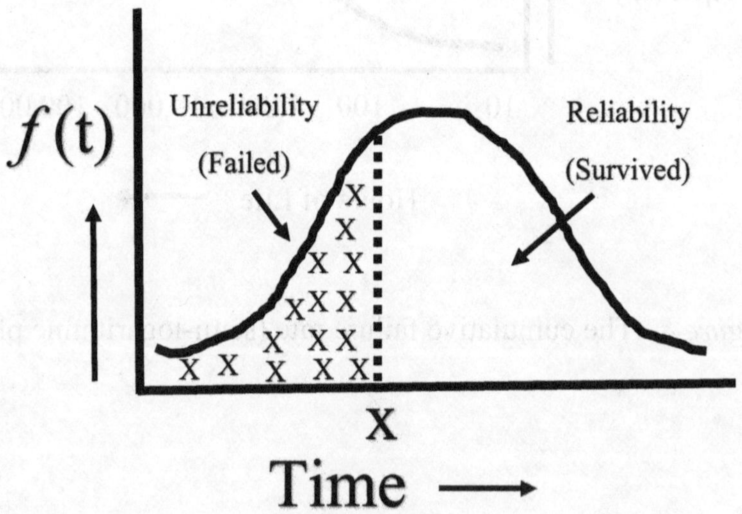

Figure 9. Unreliability + Reliability = 100%.

The survival function is the complement of the cumulative distribution function (Lyer, 2013; Marshall, 2012). The survival function $= R(t) = P(T > t) = 1 - F(t)$. See Figure 10. Initially, at time $= 0$, none of the units have failed. After the useful life of the units has ended and most have failed, there will be a few that continue to survive for an extended period of time.

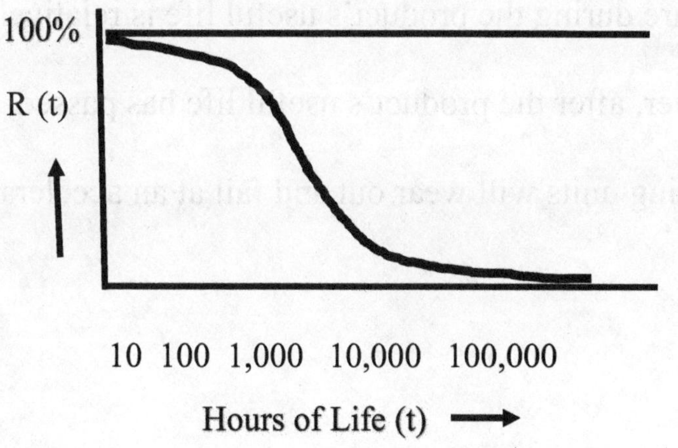

Figure 10. Survival function on semi-logarithmic plot. $R(t) = P(T > t) = 1 - P(T < t) = 1 - F(t)$.

When units are tested-to-failure, the units that have

design defects (e.g., poor quality components) will fail at

a relatively fast rate (Catalano, 1973; Marshall, 2012;

Lyer, 2013; Weibull.com, 2002, April). The number of

units that fail in this infant mortality phase can be reduced

by debugging the problems. After the weak ones have

failed and have been eliminated from the process, the rate

of failure during the product's useful life is relatively low.

However, after the product's useful life has passed, the

remaining units will wear out and fail at an accelerated

rate.

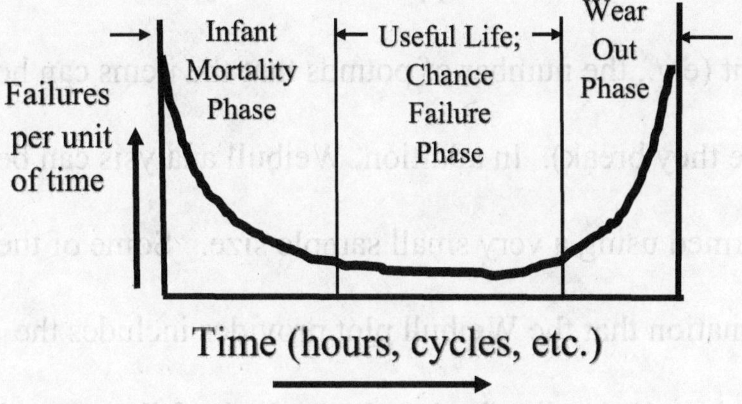

Figure 11. Failures per unit of time.

In short, Weibull analysis is useful for predicting when items will fail in the field. The units for measuring when items will fail in the field can be based on a variety of factors, such as time (e.g., the number of hours before the items fail), cycles (e.g., the number of completed rounds before the items fail), height (e.g., the number of feet that the items are dropped before they fail), and

weight (e.g., the number of pounds that the items can hold

before they break). In addition, Weibull analysis can be

performed using a very small sample size.   Some of the

information that the Weibull plot provides includes the

following: 1) the distribution shape; 2) the failure rate; 3)

the characteristic life at which 63.2% of the population

are expected to fail; 4) the life that a given percent are

expected to fail; 5) for a given percent, the confidence

interval for the true life; and 6) for a given life, the

confidence interval for the true percent failing at that life

(Ford Motor Company, 1968). In short, a Weibull plot

provides valuable information about the nature of failure

(McLinn, 1988).

CHAPTER 2

Working Through an Example Using the Weibull

Probability Plot

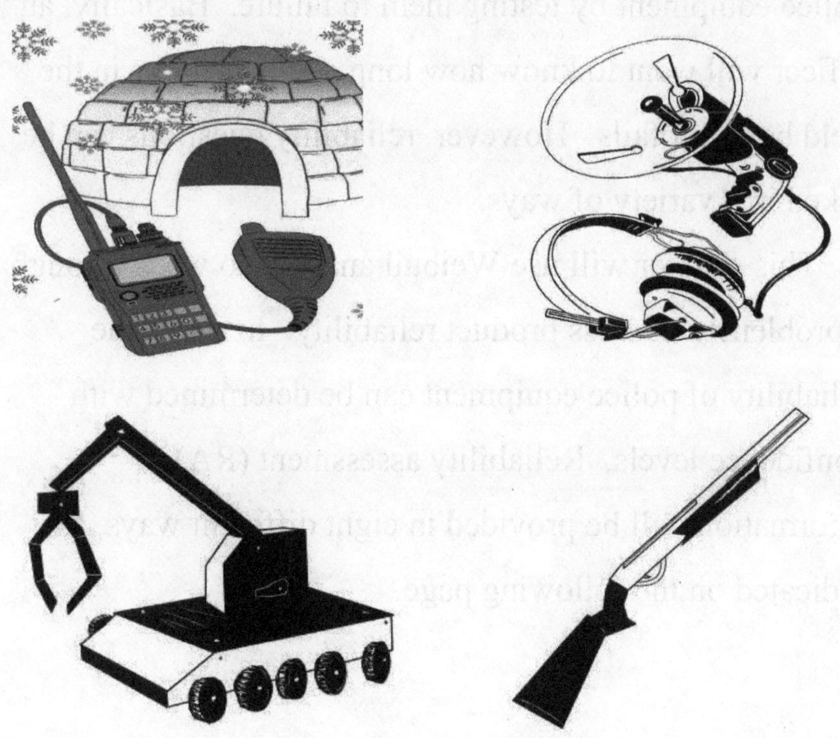

Figure 12. Various police tools that may be tested-to-failure.

Weibull Test-to-Failure Analysis: Reliability Assessment (RA)

This chapter describes how to assess the reliability of police equipment by testing them to failure. Basically, an officer will want to know how long a tool will last in the field before it fails. However, reliability questions can be asked in a variety of ways.

This chapter will use Weibull analysis to work through a problem to address product reliability. In short, the reliability of police equipment can be determined with confidence levels. Reliability assessment (RA) information will be provided in eight different ways, as indicated on the following page.

RA1) Determine the distribution shape and the failure
      rate of the tool.

RA2) Determine the characteristic life of the tool.

RA3) Determine the life that a given percentage of tools
      are expected to fail.

RA4) For a given life, determine the percentage of tools
      that are expected to fail.

RA5) Determine the confidence interval for the true life.

RA6) For a given life, determine the confidence interval
      for the true percent failing at that life.

RA7) Make a one-sided confidence statement about the
      true percent failing at a given life.

RA8) Make a one-sided confidence statement about the
      true life at a given percent failure rate.

Overview of Steps to Complete for

Reliability Assessment

1) Collect data (test the tools to failure in the environments or conditions in which they may be used). Life could be measured by the number of hours, the number of times fired, the amount of pressure, the number of feet that items are dropped, the number of pounds that the items can hold, etc. Suppose 13 items were tested, but 3 items were suspended. Suspended items are items that were removed from the test, for various reasons, before the items failed. Thus, of the 13 items tested, only 10 items were actually tested-to-failure.

2) Arrange the data in ascending order (from shortest life to longest life). Include suspended items and the times that the suspended items were removed from the test.

3) Calculate the mean order values and median rank values for the 10 failed items. The sample size for these calculations will include the suspended items (sample size = N = 13). Basically, the 3 suspended items will be adjusted into the 10 mean order values and the 10 median rank values.

4) Plot the hours-to-failure and their corresponding median ranks on Weibull probability plot paper. Draw a line-of-best fit.

5) From the Weibull plot paper, determine the Weibull slope by creating a line parallel to the line-of-best fit by transferring a parallel line to the Weibull slope indicator. The Weibull slope indicator is at the top left corner on the Weibull plot paper.

6) Use the slope to determine the distribution shape and the failure rate. **(RA 1)**

7) From the plot, determine the characteristic life. The characteristic life is the time at which 63.2% of the population are expected to fail. **(RA 2)**

8) From the plot, determine the life that a given percent are expected to fail. For a given life, determine the percent that are expected to fail.   **(RA 3; RA 4)**

9) Now consider a confidence level. Select a desired confidence level for the confidence band. Suppose a 90% confidence level has been selected.

10) Calculate the lower and upper percent ranks for the 90% confidence level. These ranks will be used to create the lower and upper rank lines, which represent the boundaries of the confidence level. For this example, suppose the lower and upper ranks have been calculated to be 5% and 95%. Notice that the 10% lack of confidence (100% - 90%) has been equally spread out on either extreme (5% failing too early and 5% never failing). For example, had a 60% confidence level been selected, the lower and upper ranks would have been 20% and 80%, respectively.

11) From a statistics book, collect the 5% and 95% confidence level rank values for a sample size of 13.

Although statistics books may provide rank values for a sample size of 13, these values do not consider suspended items. Thus, they cannot be used in this example without modification. This example started with a sample size of 13, but only 10 items were tested-to-failure. Simply using the unmodified rank values for a sample size of 10 would also be incorrect. The three suspended items cannot simply be discarded because they did survive a certain amount of time. Therefore, the rank values from a statistics book for a sample size of 13 must be collected and modified to account for the three suspended items.

12) Based on the mean order values and on the 5% and 95% rank values, interpolation must be performed to calculate the adjusted 5% confidence level rank values and adjusted 95% confidence level rank values.

13) Plot the confidence bands on Weibull probability plot paper. This can be accomplished by plotting the adjusted 5% and adjusted 95% confidence level rank values against the actual hours to failure.

14) From the plot, for a given percent, determine the confidence interval for the true life. **(RA 5)**

15) From the plot, for a given life, determine the confidence interval for the true percent failing at that life. **(RA 6)**

16) From the plot, make a one-sided confidence statement about the true percent failing at a given life. **(RA 7)**

17) From the plot, make a one-sided confidence statement about the true life at a given percent failure rate. **(RA 8)**

Thermal Chamber

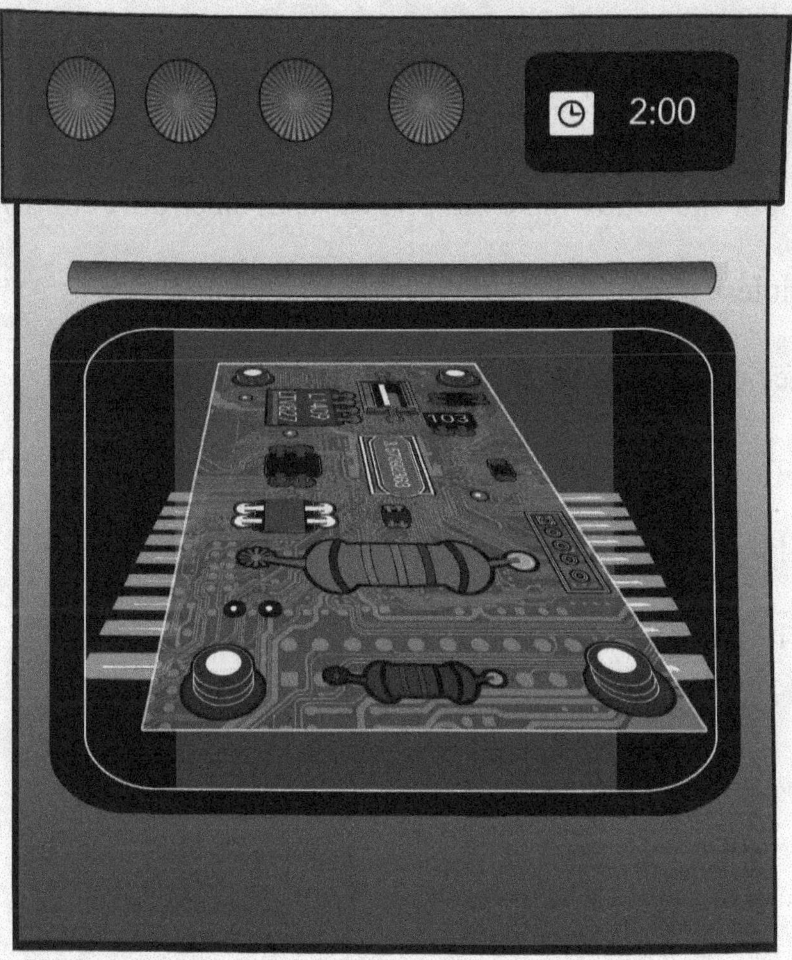

Figure 13. Electronic module placed inside a thermal chamber and tested-to-failure.

Solving a Problem: Working through the 17 steps

by using Weibull Analysis

For the following example, thirteen electronic control modules (tools), which are used in unique and harsh police environments, have been placed into a thermal chamber. See Figure 13. The modules were not removed until the items either failed or were suspended. Each of the 17 steps will be described.

Step 1. Test the items to failure. Record the times. Assume that the information in Table 1 is correct; three of the items were suspended and 10 items failed. Suspended items are items that were removed from the test, for various reasons, before the items failed.

Step 2. Arrange the data in ascending order (from shortest life to longest life). Include the times for suspended items. The number of hours when each item failed or was suspended is indicated in Table 1.

Table 1

Thirteen Items Tested; Three Items Were Removed Prior to Failure.

ITEM NUMBER	STATUS	HOURS WHEN FAILED/SUSPENDED
1	Failed	67
2	Failed	124
3	Suspended (Removed, non-failed)	145
4	Failed	161
5	Failed	185
6	Failed	217
7	Suspended (Removed, non-failed)	220
8	Failed	225
9	Failed	261
10	Suspended (Removed, non-failed)	278
11	Failed	297
12	Failed	342
13	Failed	428

Step 3. Calculate the mean order values and median rank values for the 10 failed items. The equations for determining the mean order values and median rank values depend on the sample size. The sample size for the calculations will include the suspended items (i.e., the sample size, N, equals 13 in this example).

One question that might arise is whether an exact percentile rank or approximate percentile rank is preferred. Using approximate percentile ranks (e.g., median ranks) may be preferred over using exact percentile ranks (Kapur & Lamberson, 1977; MathPages, n.d.). For example, suppose that there were 5 tools tested-to-failure and the first tool failed at 75 hours and the second tool failed at 100 hours. Using exact percentile ranks, the first failed tool at 75 hours represents a cumulative failure rate of 20% (1/5), the second failed tool at 100 hours represents a cumulative failure rate of 40% (2/5), and so on. However, this is less than optimal because statistically the first failure will most likely occur slightly before 75 hours. In addition, based on a sample size of 5, it is not likely that 100% of the population will fail prior to the failure time of the fifth tool.

To demonstrate the point, suppose there is a population of a single tool and it is tested-to-failure, which fails at time t. The cumulative distribution function gives the probability that a tool will fail before time t (Marshall, 2012; MathPages, n.d.). Hence, the expected number of failures at time t will be 0.5. In other words, there is a 0.5 probability that the failure will occur prior to time t and a 0.5 probability that the failure will occur after time t. Thus, for the first failed item for a population of one tool, the expected number of failures at the time of the first failure is only 0.5. Statistically, the first failure will most likely occur before the expected number of failures reaches one. Another problem with plotting exact percentile ranks is that the Weibull probability plot paper does not define the 100% point.

Using median ranks is an effective and widely used method for determining the cumulative percent for failed items over time (Catalano, 1973; Forgione, 1963; Weibull.com, 2002, April). However, because the median rank values depend directly on the mean order values, the mean order values must be calculated prior to the determination of the median rank values. The mean order is the sequenced order of failed items.

Referring back to Table 1, the mean order for the first failed item is one because it is the first failure (Kapur &

Lamberson, 1977). Likewise, the second failure has a

mean order of two because it is clearly the second failure.

However, the first removal (suspended item) occurred for

the third item. It is not known whether the third item

would have failed before the fourth item had the third

item been tested-to-failure and not removed. However,

because item number three was in the sample and did

survive 145 hours, it cannot be discarded.

Because the mean order and median rank are only

calculated for failed units, a mean order and median rank

will not be calculated for item number three (Ford Motor

Company, 1969; Kapur & Lamberson, 1977). However, a

suspended item will influence the mean orders and the

median ranks for the failed items following it. This will

cause the mean orders and median ranks to no longer have equal increments.

The mean order for the fourth item can be calculated by determining the average number of ways that the fourth item could have failed before and after the suspended item directly before it (Kapur & Lamberson, 1977). However, when there are many items being considered, with many of them being suspended, this can be overwhelming. As a more practical solution, there is a general formula for calculating incremental mean order values. Once an incremental mean order value is calculated, the same increment will be used until another suspended item is encountered. An incremental value is used to increase the mean order values for consecutive

failures. The general formula is described below.

New increment for **Mean Order** =

$$\frac{(N + 1) - (\textit{previous mean order number})}{1 + (\textit{number of items beyond present suspended item})},$$

where N = sample size, which includes suspended

items.

Once the mean order values have been calculated, the

corresponding median rank values can be calculated. The

exact calculation for the median rank values can be quite

complicated. Therefore, a practical approximate formula

for calculating the median rank is described below

(Dodson, 2006; Forgione, 1963; Kapur & Lamberson,

1977).

$$\text{Median Rank Estimator} = \frac{M - 0.3}{N + 0.4},$$

where M = Mean Order Number

and

N = Sample Size, which includes suspended items.

Using the mean order and median rank equations, Tables

2 - 4 can be constructed.

Table 2

Determining Mean Order Values. N = 13.

Item Number	Status	Failed Item	Mean Order Increment for N = 13	Mean Order Value
1	Failed	1	1	1
2	Failed	2	1	2
3	Suspended (Removed, non-failure)	-	$\dfrac{(13+1) - 2}{1 +10} = 1.09$	-
4	Failed	3	1.09	3.09
5	Failed	4	1.09	4.18
6	Failed	5	1.09	5.27
7	Suspended (Removed, non-failure)	-	$\dfrac{(13+1) - 5.27}{1 +6} = 1.25$	-
8	Failed	6	1.25	6.52
9	Failed	7	1.25	7.77
10	Suspended (Removed, non-failure)	-	$\dfrac{(13+1) - 7.77}{1 +3} = 1.56$	-
11	Failed	8	1.56	9.33
12	Failed	9	1.56	10.89
13	Failed	10	1.56	12.45

Table 3

Determining Median Rank Values. N = 13.

Failed Item Number	Status	Mean Order Value (M)	Median Rank = $\frac{M - 0.3}{N + 0.4}$	Median Rank (%)
1	Failed	1	$\frac{(1 - 0.3)}{(13 + 0.4)} = .052$	5.2
2	Failed	2	$\frac{(2 - 0.3)}{(13 + 0.4)} = .127$	12.7
3	Failed	3.09	$\frac{(3.09 - 0.3)}{(13 + 0.4)} = .208$	20.8
4	Failed	4.18	$\frac{(4.18 - 0.3)}{(13 + 0.4)} = .290$	29.0
5	Failed	5.27	$\frac{(5.27 - 0.3)}{(13 + 0.4)} = .371$	37.1
6	Failed	6.52	$\frac{(6.52 - 0.3)}{(13 + 0.4)} = .464$	46.4
7	Failed	7.77	$\frac{(7.77 - 0.3)}{(13 + 0.4)} = .557$	55.7
8	Failed	9.33	$\frac{(9.33 - 0.3)}{(13 + 0.4)} = .674$	67.4
9	Failed	10.89	$\frac{(10.89 - 0.3)}{(13 + 0.4)} = .790$	79.0
10	Failed	12.45	$\frac{(12.45 - 0.3)}{(13 + 0.4)} = .907$	90.7

Table 4

Summary Table of Ten Failed Items with Corresponding Mean Orders and Median Ranks.

FAILED ITEM	HOURS to FAILURE	MEAN ORDER	MEDIAN RANK (%)
1	67	1	5.2
2	124	2	12.7
3	161	3.09	20.8
4	185	4.18	29.0
5	217	5.27	37.1
6	225	6.52	46.4
7	261	7.77	55.7
8	297	9.33	67.4
9	342	10.89	79.0
10	428	12.45	90.7

Discussion involving Tables 4-5

Notice that the median rank values that were calculated in Table 4 for the 10 failed items do not match the median rank values in statistics books for a sample size of 10. The reason for this is that the median rank values in statistics books represent samples with no suspended items (i.e., based only on positive integer mean orders). If no items are suspended during the test, then the ordered number for each failed item (mean order) will be a positive integer, as indicated in Table 5.

Table 5

The Mean Order Will Equal the Ordered Failure Number, If There Are No Suspended Items in the Sample.

Item # (Ordered Failure, N = 10)	Mean Order (if no items are suspended)
1	1
2	2
3	3
4	4
5	5
6	6
7	7
8	8
9	9
10	10

Discussion involving Tables 6 -7

Accuracy of the Median Rank Estimator

&

Impact of Suspended Items on Median Ranks

Table 6 compares the values from a statistics book for a sample size of 10 to the estimated median rank values that were calculated for a sample size of 10 with no suspended items. This demonstrates the accuracy of the median rank estimator. Table 7 compares the impact of the three suspended items on the median ranks.

Table 6

Accuracy of the Median Rank Estimator. With No Suspended Items, the Median Ranks from a Statistics Book are Compared to the Calculated Median Ranks.

N = 10; Order of Failure = Mean Order (M)	Median Ranks (%) of 10 Items from a statistics book (Kapur & Lamberson, 1977, p. 486)	Calculated Median Ranks (%) of 10 Items Median rank = $\frac{M - 0.3}{N + 0.4}$
1	6.7	0.7 / 10.4 = 6.7
2	16.2	1.7 / 10.4 = 16.3
3	25.9	2.7/10.4 = 26.0
4	35.5	3.7/10.4 = 35.6
5	45.2	4.7/10.4 = 45.2
6	54.8	5.7/10.4 = 54.8
7	64.5	6.7/10.4 = 64.4
8	74.1	7.7/10.4 = 74.0
9	83.8	8.7/10.4 = 83.7
10	93.3	9.7/10.4 = 93.3

Table 7

Comparing the Impact of the 3 Suspended Items on the Median Ranks.

Failed Items (Mean Order if no suspended items)	Median Ranks (%) of 10 Items with no Suspended Items (Kapur & Lamberson, 1977, p. 486)	Median Ranks (%) of 10 Failed Items (with 3 Suspended Items)
1	6.7	5.2
2	16.2	12.7
3	25.9	20.8
4	35.5	29.0
5	45.2	37.1
6	54.8	46.4
7	64.5	55.7
8	74.1	67.4
9	83.8	79.0
10	93.3	90.7

Step 4. From Table 4, plot the hours-to-failure and their corresponding median ranks on Weibull probability plot paper. Draw a line-of-best fit.

Because the three suspended items are now part of the calculations, the results in Table 4 can now be plotted as if there were only 10 items in the sample. Once the Weibull line is plotted, useful information can be determined. The Weibull line can be constructed by plotting the hours-to-failure versus the median rank (%) on Weibull plot paper (Ford Motor Company, 1968). A line-of-best fit can be generated by using the last plotted data point as reference and creating a line through the points such that the number of points above and below the line are equal (King, 1971). The result is shown in Figure 14.

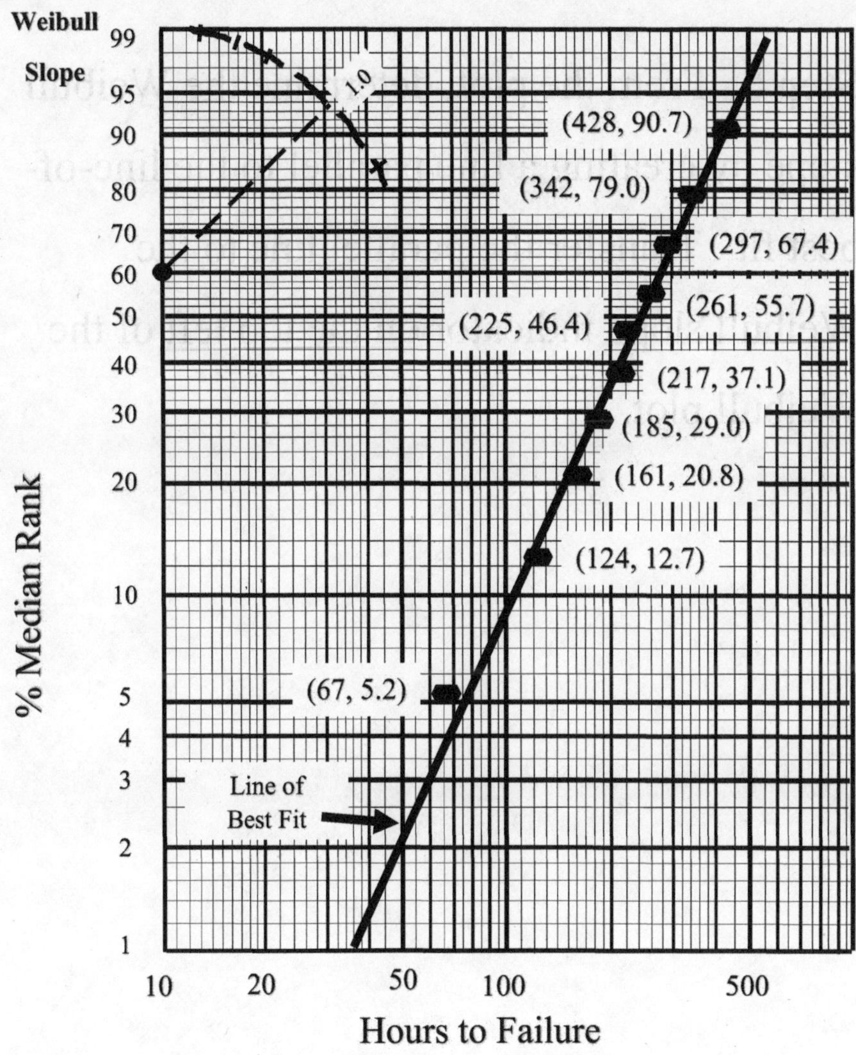

Figure 14. Weibull probability plot and line-of-best fit. Data values are from Table 4.

Step 5. From the plot, determine the Weibull slope by creating a line parallel to the line-of-best fit. Transfer the parallel line to the Weibull slope indicator on the top left of the Weibull plot.

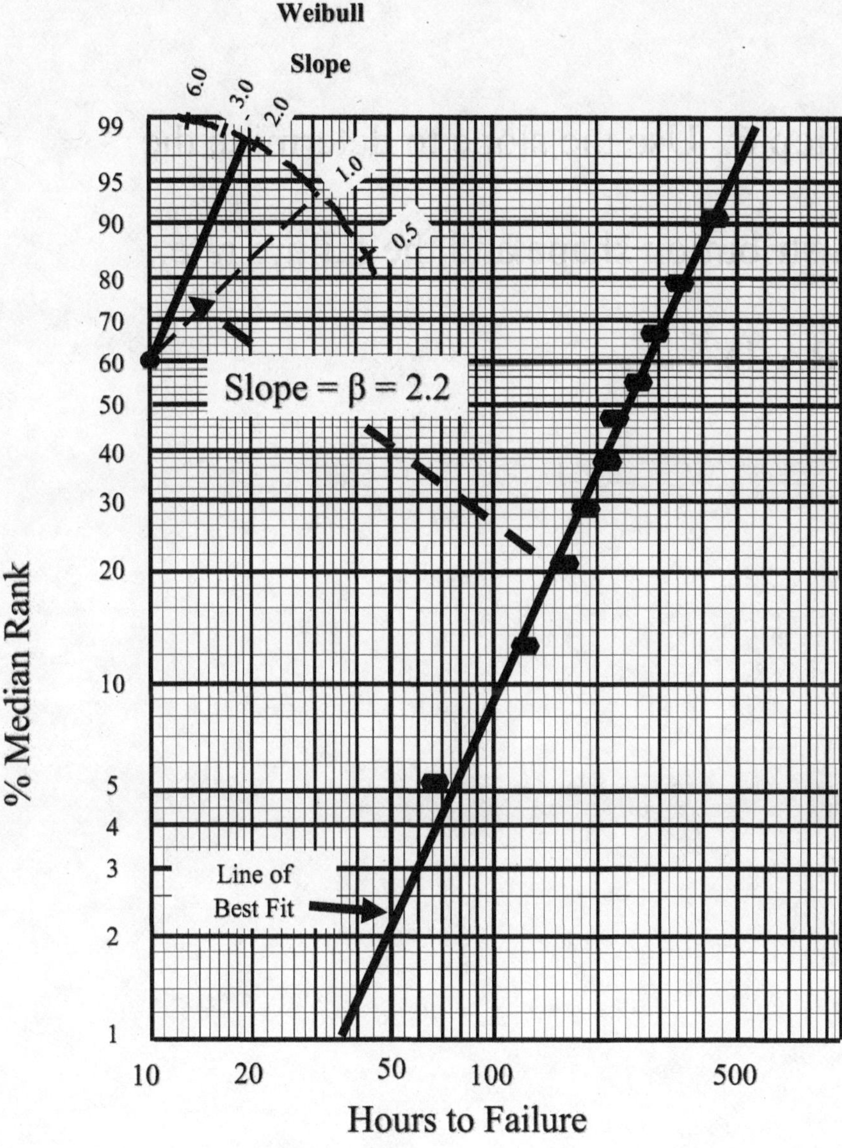

Figure 15. Weibull slope.

Step 6. Use the slope to determine the

distribution shape and the failure rate.

(RA 1)

Because the plotted data produced a straight line, the data can be modelled by the Weibull distribution (Catalano, 1973). As indicated in Figure 15, for this exercise, the Weibull slope **(β) = 2.2**. Use the information below and Figure 16 and Figure 17 to assess the shape of the Weibull distribution and the item's failure rate (Catalano, 1973; Marshall, 2012; Weibull.com, 2002, April).

If β < 1, then the data show a decreasing hazard function (e.g., infant mortality, weak components)

If β = 1, then the data show a constant hazard function (e.g., useful life of product)

If β > 1, then the data show an increasing hazard function (e.g., wear-out; product reaching end of life)

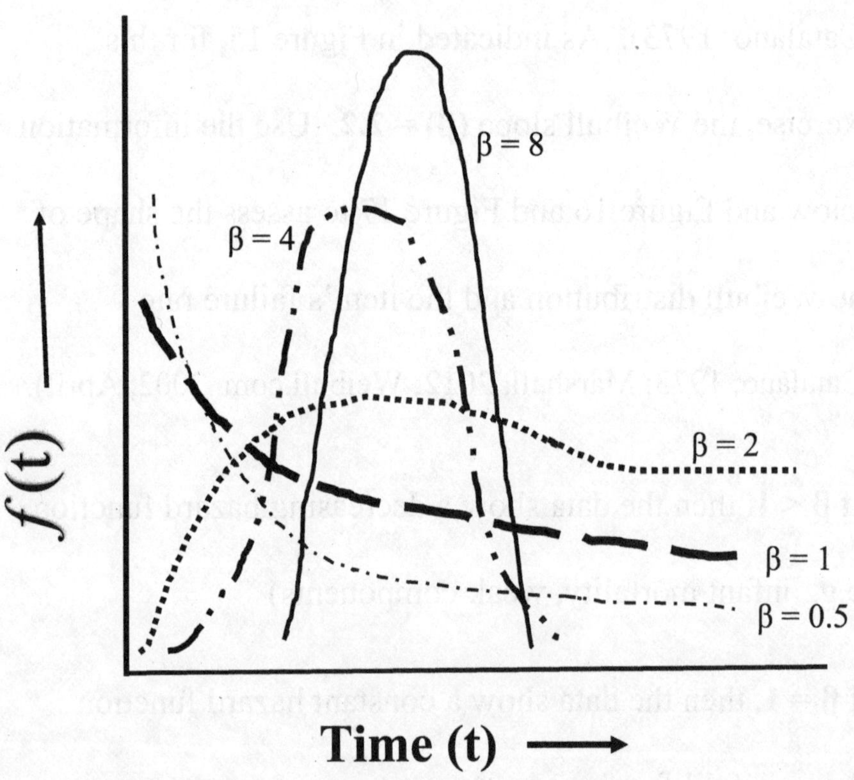

Figure 16. The Weibull distribution (density) for different values of β on normal graph paper.

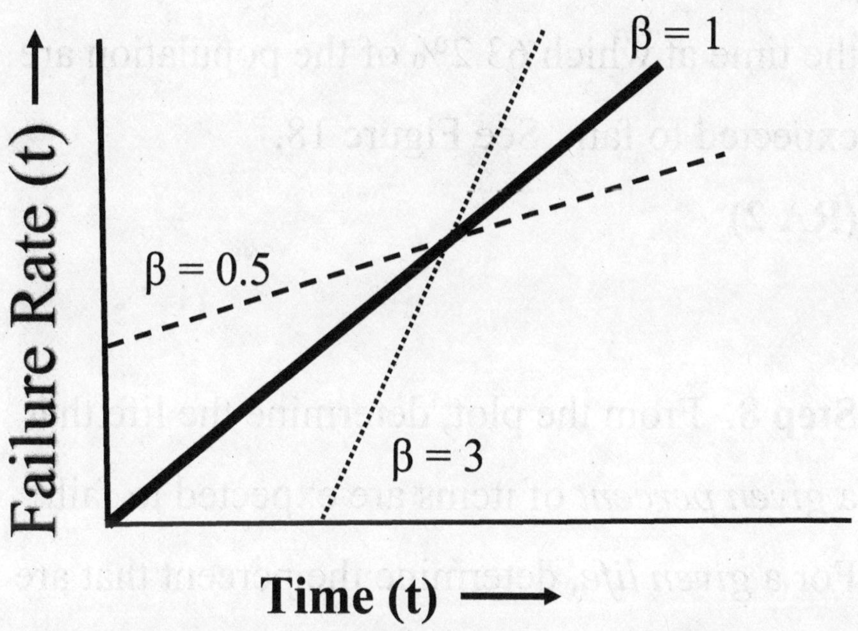

Figure 17. Failure rate for different values of β on Weibull probability plot paper.

Step 7. From the plot, determine the characteristic life. The characteristic life is the time at which 63.2% of the population are expected to fail. See Figure 18.

(RA 2)

Step 8. From the plot, determine the life that a *given percent* of items are expected to fail. For a *given life*, determine the percent that are expected to fail.   See Figure 18.

(RA 3; RA 4)

From Figure 18, the number of hours that a given

percent of items are expected to fail can be determined.

For example, in order to determine the number of hours in

which 10% of the items are expected to fail, find the point

where the 10% Median Rank line (y-axis) intersects with

the Line-of-Best fit. Then locate the corresponding

number of Hours to Failure on the x-axis. In this case,

10% of the items are expected to fail within 104 hours.

The relationship works both ways. At a given life of 104

hours, 10% of the items are expected to fail.

Apply the same technique for the characteristic life,

which is the time that 63.2% of the population are

expected to fail. Find the point where the 63.2% Median

Rank line (y-axis) intersects with the Line-of-Best fit.

Then locate the corresponding number of Hours to Failure on the x-axis. In this case, 63.2% of the items are expected to fail within 280 hours. The relationship works both ways. At a given life of 280 hours, 63.2% of the items are expected to fail.

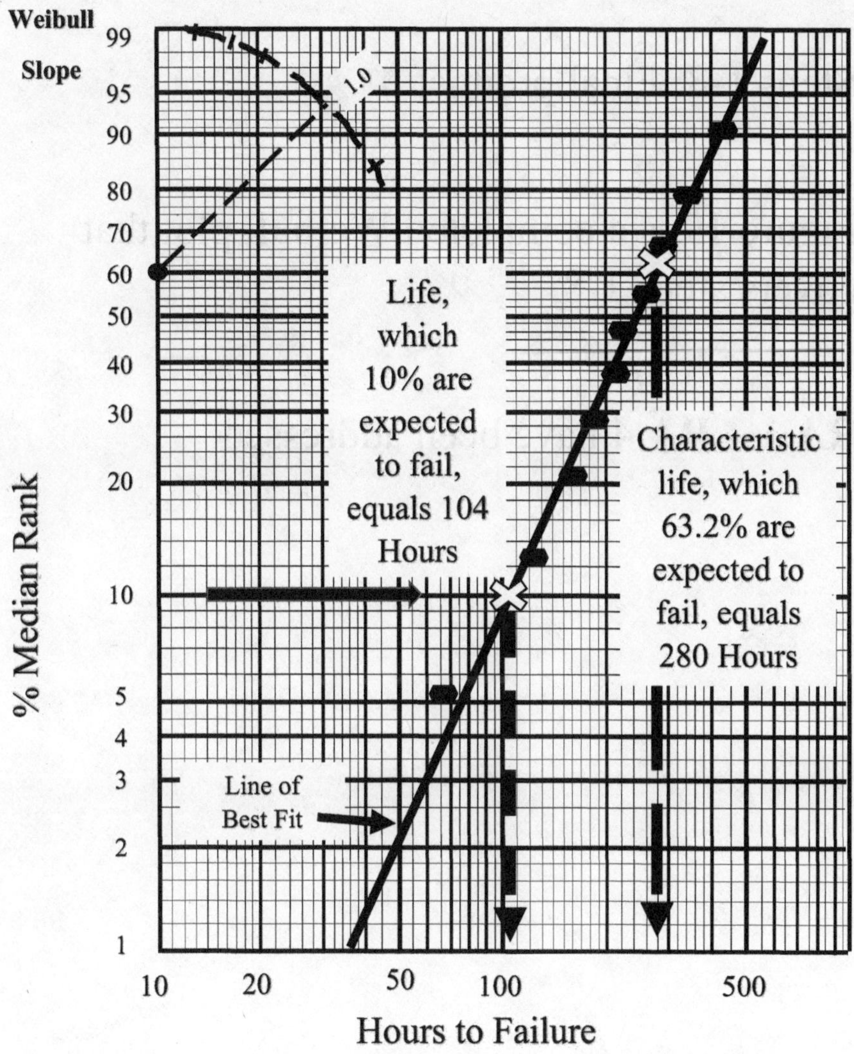

Figure 18. Ten percent of the items are expected to fail within 104 hours. The characteristic life = 280 hours.

Steps 1-8: Final product.

Figure 19 is a completed Weibull plot that covers steps 1-8.

RA 1 – RA 4 have been addressed.

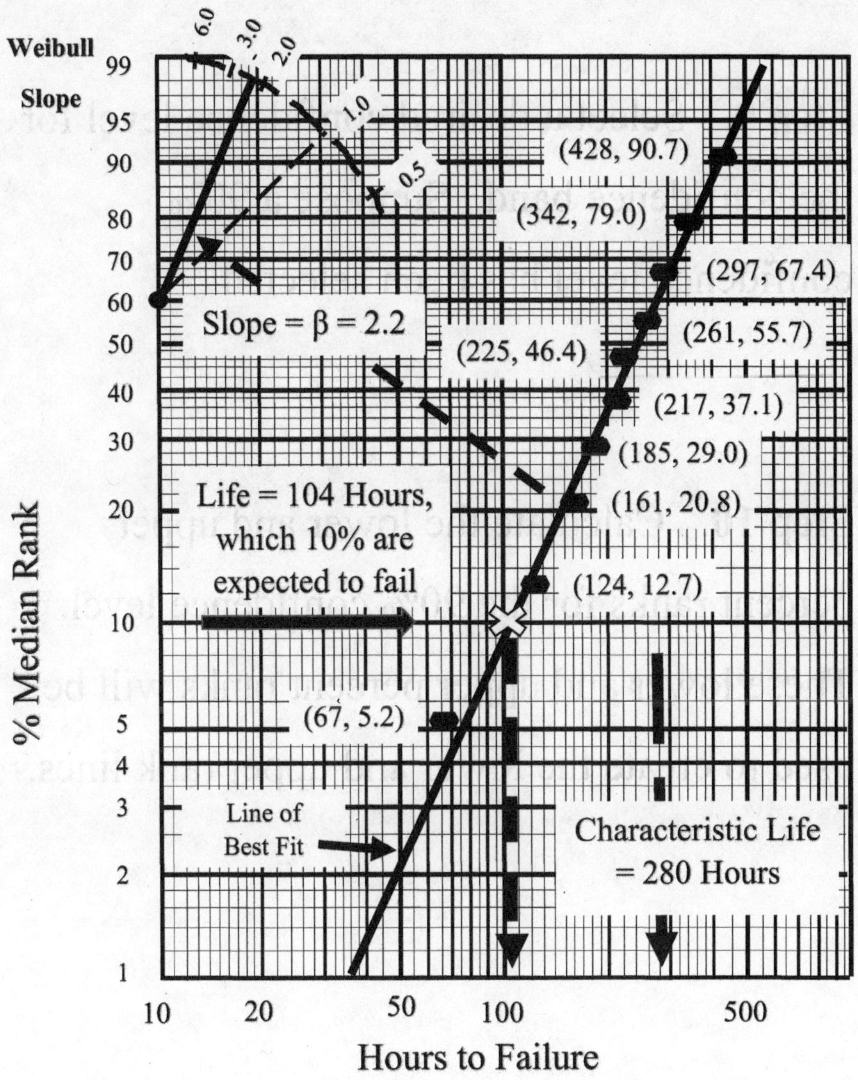

Figure 19. Completed Weibull plot that covers steps 1-8 and RA 1 - RA 4.

67

Step 9.   Select a desired confidence level for the confidence band. Suppose a 90% confidence level has been selected.

Step 10.   Calculate the lower and upper percent ranks for the 90% confidence level. These lower and upper percent ranks will be used to create the lower and upper rank lines.

Plotting the Confidence Bands

A confidence interval is a range of values that describes how precisely a statistic estimates a parameter within a margin of error (Carlberg, 2011). Suppose a 90% confidence level has been selected as the standard. The first and second rank values for the confidence interval can be calculated by using the following formulas (Ford Motor Company, 1968; Kapur & Lamberson, 1977).

First Rank Value =

$$\frac{[100\% - (\text{selected confidence factor }\%)]}{2}$$

and the

Second Rank Value =

$$\frac{[100\% + (\text{selected confidence factor }\%)]}{2}.$$

Therefore, the

First Rank Value = (100% - 90%) / 2 = 5%

and the

Second Rank Value = (100% + 90%) / 2 = 95%.

The 5% and 95% rank values that will establish a confidence band for a sample size of 13 can be found in statistical books (Kapur & Lamberson, 1977). A sample size of 13 is required because that is the number of items in the original sample (10 failed items plus 3 suspended items). It would be improper to use the 5% and 95% rank values for a sample size of 10 from a statistics book because the values in the book do not account for suspended items. Thus, the 5% and 95% rank values for a sample size of 13 will need to be collected and adjusted for the 10 failed items in this exercise to account for the three suspended items.

Step 11. From a statistics book, collect the 5% and 95% confidence level rank values for a sample size of 13.

Remember, the sample size represents an ordered failure and the rank values correspond to the ordered failure.

Table 8

5% and 95% Confidence Level Rank Values for N = 13.

Sample Size	5% Ranks (Kapur & Lamberson, 1977, p. 490)	95% Ranks (Kapur & Lamberson, 1977, p. 494)
1	.394	20.582
2	2.805	31.634
3	6.605	41.010
4	11.267	49.465
5	16.566	57.262
6	22.395	64.520
7	28.705	71.295
8	35.480	77.604
9	42.738	83.434
10	50.535	88.733
11	58.990	93.395
12	68.366	97.195
13	79.418	99.606

Step 12. Due to the influence of the three

suspended items, adjust the 5% and 95%

confidence level rank values.

Remember, if no items were suspended, then the mean order will equal the ordered failure. However, once a suspended item is encountered, subsequent mean orders will need to be adjusted. As stated earlier, the 5% and 95% confidence level rank values from the statistics book do not account for suspended items. Indeed, there would be too many possible combinations of suspended and failed items to consider (Kapur & Lamberson, 1977). In short, the 5% and 95% confidence level rank values indicated in Table 8 are based on positive mean order integers and will need to be adjusted to account for the three suspended items.

Only the rank values for failed items will be determined; only failed items are plotted on Weibull plot paper (Forgione, 1963; King, 1971). The mean orders for

the 10 failed items have already been adjusted to account

for the three suspended items. However, the 5% and 95%

confidence level rank values that correspond to the

adjusted mean order values have not been established.

Because some of the mean orders in this example are not

integers, their corresponding 5% and 95% adjusted

confidence level rank values will need to be determined

by interpolation. Table 9 and Table 10 provide a quick

estimate of the expected values for the 5% and 95%

adjusted confidence level rank values.

Table 9

Ten Failed Items, Adjusted Mean Orders, and a Quick Estimate of the Range for the 5% Adjusted Confidence Level Rank Values.

Failed items	Adjusted Mean Orders, which account for suspended items	Based on Table 8 (N = 13), Quick Estimate of Adjusted **5%** Confidence Level Ranks for 10 Failed Items; x = adjusted rank value based on the adjusted Mean Order (will need to interpolate)
1	1.0	.394
2	2.0	2.805
3	3.09	6.605 < x < 11.267
4	4.18	11.267 < x < 16.566
5	5.27	16.566 < x < 22.395
6	6.52	22.395 < x < 28.705
7	7.77	28.705 < x < 35.480
8	9.33	42.738 < x < 50.535
9	10.89	50.535 < x < 58.990
10	12.45	68.366 < x < 79.418

Table 10

Ten Failed Items, Adjusted Mean Orders, and a Quick Estimate of the Range for the 95% Adjusted Confidence Level Rank Values.

Failed items	Adjusted Mean Orders, which account for suspended items	Based on Table 8 (N = 13), Quick Estimate of Adjusted **95%** Confidence Level Ranks for 10 Failed Items; x = adjusted rank value based on the adjusted Mean Order (will need to interpolate)
1	1.0	20.582
2	2.0	31.634
3	3.09	41.010 < x < 49.465
4	4.18	49.465 < x < 57.262
5	5.27	57.262 < x < 64.520
6	6.52	64.520 < x < 71.295
7	7.77	71.295 < x < 77.604
8	9.33	83.434 < x < 88.733
9	10.89	88.733 < x < 93.395
10	12.45	97.195 < x < 99.606

As shown in Tables 9 – 10, the adjusted confidence

level rank values will be within a range of lower and

upper rank values. Each lower and upper rank value

corresponds to a specific positive mean order integer.

Statistics books only provide the lower and upper rank

values associated with positive mean order integers

(Kapur & Lamberson, 1977). Because not all of the

adjusted mean order values in this example are positive

integers, interpolation is required to determine the

adjusted confidence level rank values.

The calculations, in this example, use the lower rank

values as the reference points. In other words, an

incremental change in a rank value represents an increase

from the lower rank value. Notice that for item 10, which

has an adjusted mean order of 12.45, the range will be

determined by the rank values associated with ordered

failed items 12 and 13 (12 < 12.45 < 13). The following

explains how to calculate the adjusted confidence level

rank values for the 10 failed items.

Formula for 5% and 95% adjusted confidence level rank values (ARV):

$$\text{ARV} = \text{lower rank value} + \frac{(\Delta \text{ rank value}) (\Delta \text{ mean order})}{\Delta \text{ failed item number}}$$

Another way of expressing the equation is listed below.

$$ARV = B_X + \frac{[(B_{(X+1)} - B_X)(C_X - A_X)]}{(A_{(X+1)} - A_X)}$$

where

ARV = 5% (or 95%) adjusted confidence level rank value

A_X = Adjusted mean order value truncated down to positive

integer (or closest positive integer less than C_X)

$A_{(X+1)}$ = A_X + 1 (or closest positive integer greater than C_X)

B_X = 5% (or 95%) rank value associated with the positive

integer A_X

$B_{(X+1)}$ = 5% (or 95%) rank value associated with the positive

integer $A_{(X+1)}$

C_X = Adjusted mean order value

The information is summarized in Tables 11 – 13.

Table 11

Adjusted 5% Confidence Level Rank Values.

Sample Size = 13 (Needed for rank values)	5% Ranks (Kapur & Lamberson, 1977, p. 490)	Adjusted Mean Order	Failed items	Calculations for Determining 5% Adjusted Confidence Level Rank Values (ARV)	5% Adjusted Confidence Level Rank Values
A_X	B_X	C_X		$B_X + [\,(B_{(X+1)} - B_X)\,(C_X - A_X)\,]\,/$ $(A_{(X+1)} - A_X)$	
1	.394	1	1	-	.394
2	2.805	2	2	-	2.805
3	6.605	3.09	3	6.605 + [(11.267 - 6.605) (3.09 – 3)] / (4 – 3)	7.025
4	11.267	4.18	4	11.267 + [(16.566 – 11.267) (4.18 - 4)] / (5 – 4)	12.221
5	16.566	5.27	5	16.566 + [(22.395 – 16.566) (5.27 - 5)] / (6 – 5)	18.140

6	22.395	6.52	6	$22.395 + [(28.705 - 22.395)(6.52 - 6)] / (7 - 6)$	25.676
7	28.705	7.77	7	$28.705 + [(35.480 - 28.705)(7.77 - 7)] / (8 - 7)$	33.922
8	35.480	9.33	8	$42.738 + [(50.535 - 42.738)(9.33 - 9)] / (10 - 9)$	45.311
9	42.738				
10	50.535	10.89	9	$50.535 + [(58.990 - 50.535)(10.89 - 10)] / (11 - 10)$	58.060
11	58.990				
12	68.366	12.45	10	$68.366 + [(79.418 - 68.366)(12.45 - 12)] / (13 - 12)$	73.339
13	79.418				

Table 12

Adjusted 95% Confidence Level Rank Values.

Sample Size = 13 (Needed for rank values)	95% Ranks (Kapur & Lamberson, 1977, p. 494)	Adjusted Mean Order	Failed items	Calculations for Determining 95% Adjusted Confidence Level Rank Values	95% Adjusted Confidence Level Rank Values
A_X	B_X	C_X		$B_X + [\,(B_{(X+1)} - B_X)\,(C_X - A_X)]\,/\,[(A_{(X+1)} - A_X]$	
1	20.582	1	1	-	20.582
2	31.634	2	2	-	31.634
3	41.010	3.09	3	$41.010 + [(49.465 - 41.010)\,(3.09 - 3)]\,/\,(4-3)$	41.771
4	49.465	4.18	4	$49.465 + [(57.262 - 49.465)\,(4.18 - 4)]\,/\,(5-4)$	50.868
5	57.262	5.27	5	$57.262 + [(64.520 - 57.262)\,(5.27 - 5)]\,/\,(6-5)$	59.222

6	64.520	6.52	6	$64.520 + [(71.295 - 64.520)(6.52 - 6)] / (7 - 6)$	68.043
7	71.295	7.77	7	$71.295 + [(77.604 - 71.295)(7.77 - 7)] / (8 - 7)$	76.153
8	77.604	9.33	8	$83.434 + [(88.733 - 83.434)(9.33 - 9)] / (10 - 9)$	85.183
9	83.434				
10	88.733	10.89	9	$88.733 + [(93.395 - 88.733)(10.89 - 10)] / (11 - 10)$	92.882
11	93.395				
12	97.195	12.45	10	$97.195 + [(99.606 - 97.195)(12.45 - 12)] / (13 - 12)$	98.280
13	99.606				

Table 13

Ten Failed Items with Corresponding Mean Orders, Median Ranks, and Adjusted Confidence Level Rank Values.

FAILED ITEM	ACTUAL HOURS	MEAN ORDER	MEDIAN RANK (%)	ADJUSTED CONFIDENCE LEVEL RANK VALUES	
				5% Ranks	95% Ranks
1	67	1	5.2	.39	20.58
2	124	2	12.7	2.81	31.63
3	161	3.09	20.8	7.03	41.77
4	185	4.18	29.0	12.22	50.87
5	217	5.27	37.1	18.14	59.22
6	225	6.52	46.4	25.68	68.04
7	261	7.77	55.7	33.92	76.15
8	297	9.33	67.4	45.31	85.18
9	342	10.89	79.0	58.06	92.88
10	428	12.45	90.6	73.34	98.28

Step 13. Plot the confidence bands on Weibull probability plot paper for the 10 failed items. This is accomplished by plotting the adjusted 5% and 95% rank values against the actual hours to failure (Kapur & Lamberson, 1977). Remember, the confidence bands should not be extended much beyond the plotted points (Ford Motor Company, 1968; Kapur & Lamberson, 1977).

See Table 14 and Figure 20.

Table 14

Actual Hours to Failure and 5% and 95% Adjusted Confidence Level Rank Values.

FAILED ITEM	ACTUAL HOURS to FAILURE	ADJUSTED CONFIDENCE LEVEL RANK VALUES	
		5%	**95%**
1	67	.39	20.58
2	124	2.81	31.63
3	161	7.03	41.77
4	185	12.22	50.87
5	217	18.14	59.22
6	225	25.68	68.04
7	261	33.92	76.15
8	297	45.31	85.18
9	342	58.06	92.88
10	428	73.34	98.28

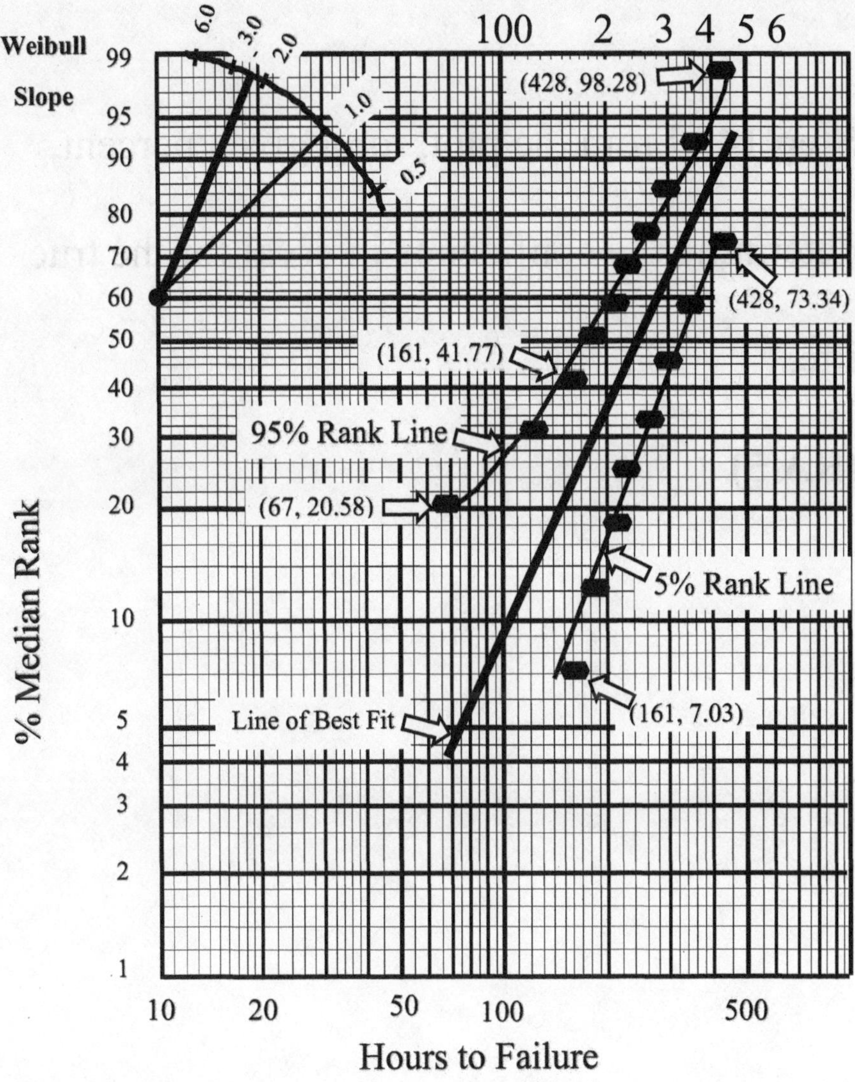

Figure 20. Confidence interval. The 5% and 95% rank lines represent the 5% and 95% adjusted confidence level rank values.

89

Step 14. From the plot, for a given percent,

determine the confidence interval for the true

life.

(RA 5)

Assume that the investigator wants to know the 90% confidence interval for the number of hours when no more than 20% of the items are expected to fail.

Find the points where the 20% Median Rank line (y-axis) intersects with the 95% and 5% confidence bands. See Figure 21.

74 hours $\leq$

true life when no more than 20% are expected to fail

$$\leq \textbf{213 hours.}$$

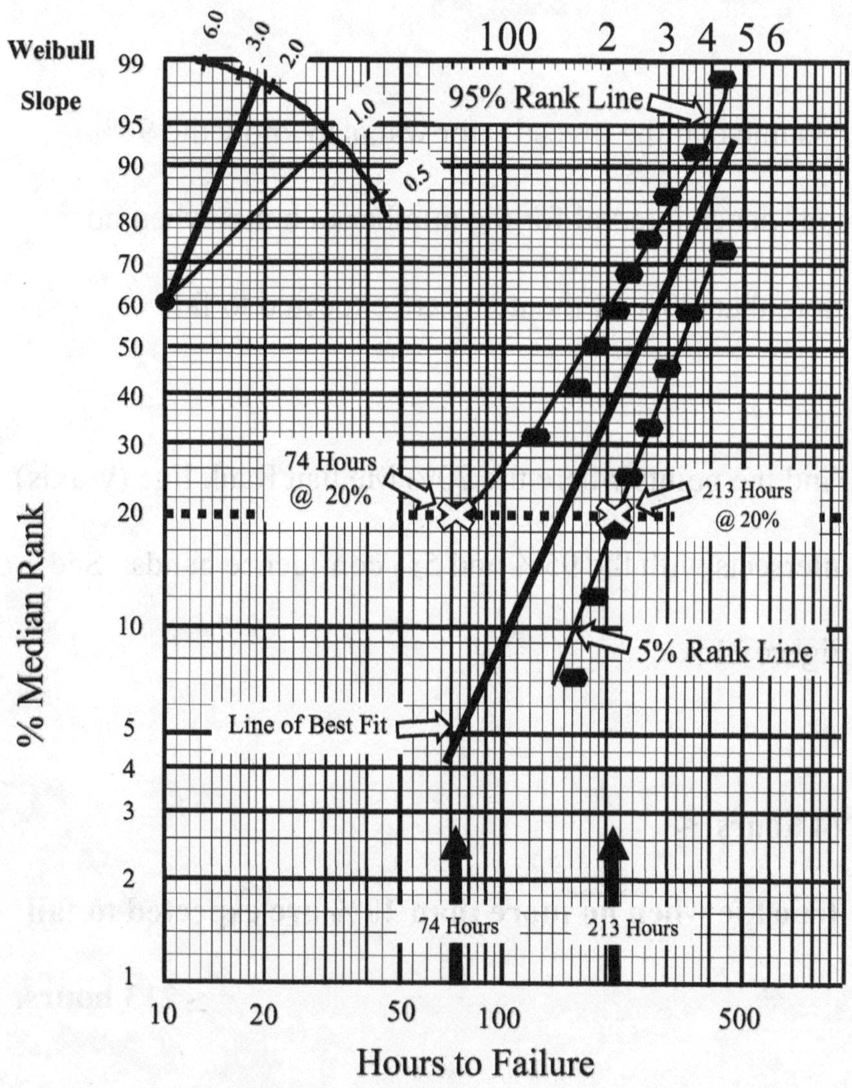

Figure 21. 74 hours ≤ true life where no more than 20% are expected to fail ≤ 213 hours.

Step 15. From the plot, at a given life, determine the confidence interval for the true percent failing at that life. This is done by intersecting the vertical line of the given life value with the 5% and 95% confidence rank lines. See Figure 22.

(RA 6)

Assume that the investigator wants to know the 90% confidence interval for the true percent failing at 300 hours.

Find the points where 300 hours-to-failure line intersects with the 95% and 5% confidence rank lines. See Figure 22.

The true percent failing at 300 hours is described below.

43 % $\leq$ failure rate at 300 hours $\leq$ 82%.

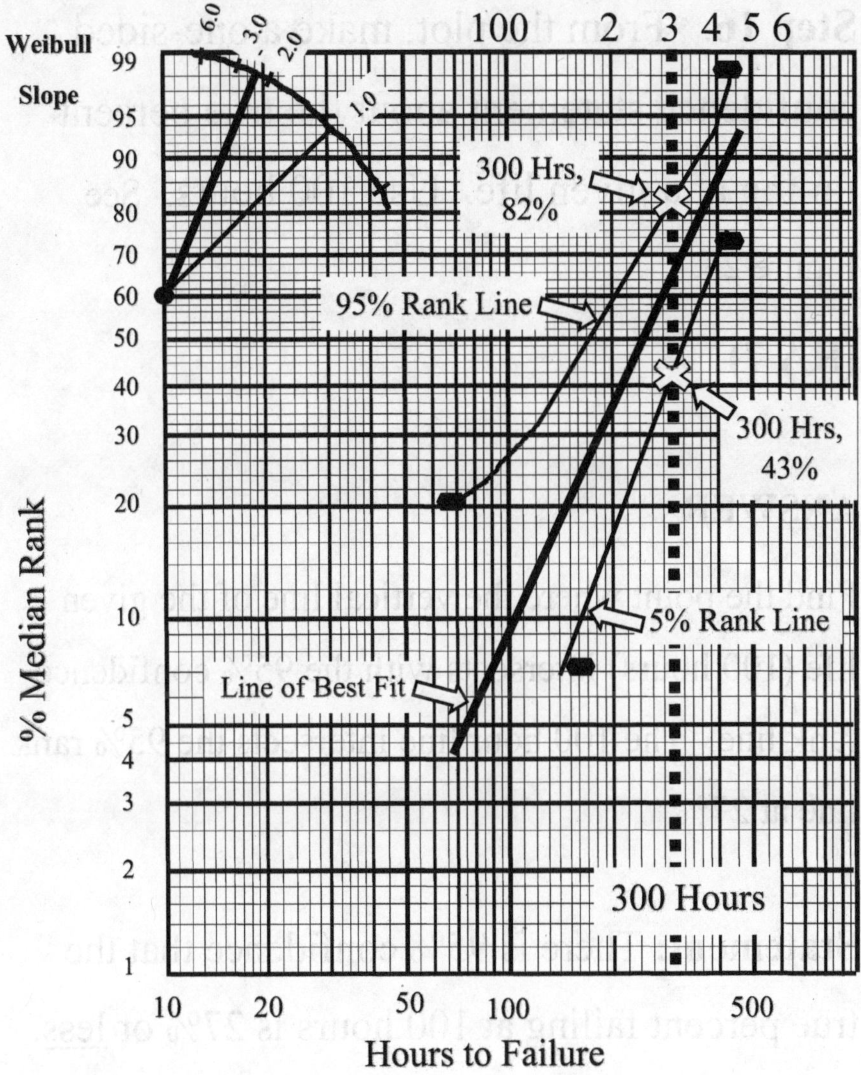

Figure 22. True percent failing at 300 hours.

43 % ≤ failure rate at 300 hours ≤ 82%.

95

Step 16.   From the plot, make a one-sided confidence statement about the true percent failing at a given life. Use 100 hours. See Figure 23.

(RA 7)

ANSWER

Find the point where the vertical line of the given life (100 hours) intersects with the 95% confidence rank line. The 100 hour line intersects the 95% rank line at 27%.

Statement: There is 95% confidence that the true percent failing at 100 hours is 27% or <u>less</u>.

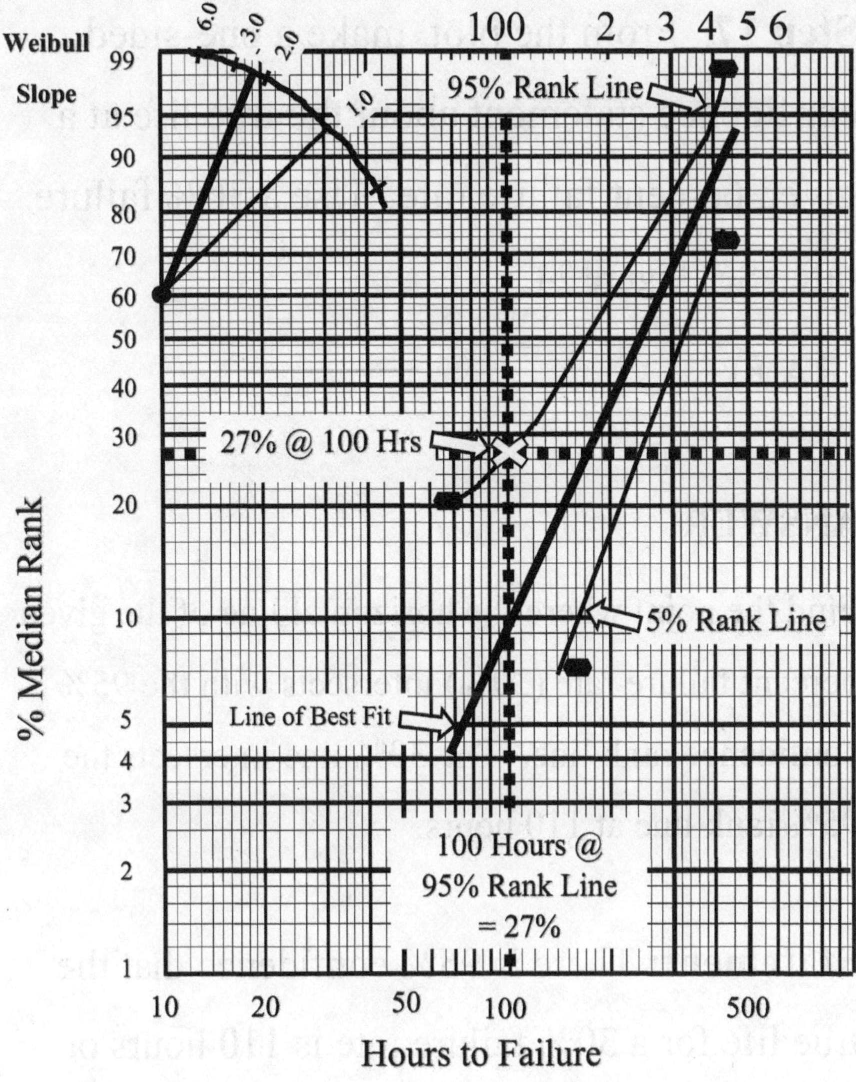

Figure 23. One-sided confidence statement about the true percent failing at a given life.

Step 17. From the plot, make a one-sided confidence statement about the true life at a given percent failure rate. Use a 30% failure rate. See Figure 24.

(RA 8)

ANSWER

Find the point where the horizontal line of the given percent failure rate (30%) intersects with the 95% confidence rank line. The 30% line intersects the 95% rank line at 110 hours.

Statement: There is 95% confidence that the true life for a 30% failure rate is 110 hours or <u>greater</u>.

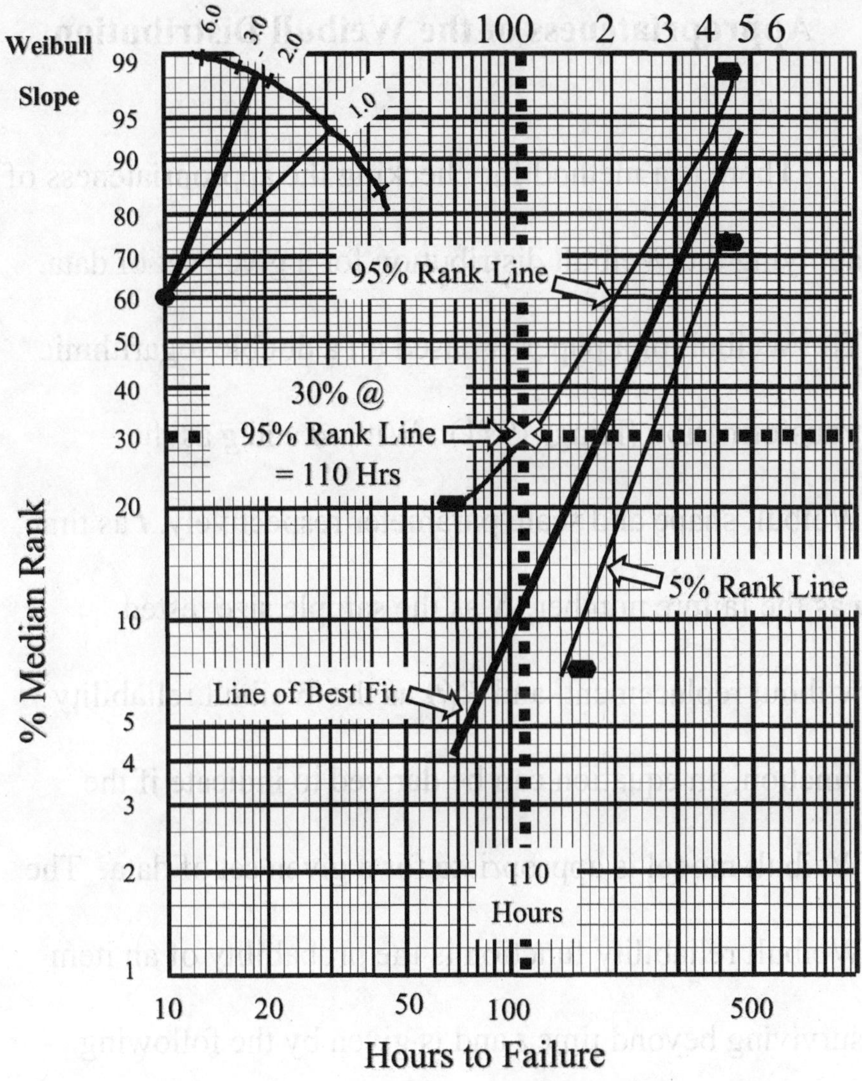

Figure 24. One-sided confidence statement about the true life at a given percent failure rate.

Appropriateness of the Weibull Distribution

There is a method for checking the appropriateness of applying the Weibull distribution for a given set of data. The Weibull plot paper is based on a double logarithmic transformation (King, 1971). With *m* and *g* as the Weibull shape and scale parameter respectively, *t* as time, *i* as the failure number, *N* as the sample size tested without replacement, and *R(t)* as the Weibull reliability function, an equation can be derived to indicate if the Weibull model is appropriate for a given set of data. The Weibull reliability function is the probability of an item surviving beyond time *t* and is given by the following equation (Chatfield, 1983).

$$R(t) = \exp[-gt^m]. \tag{1}$$

Taking the natural logarithmic of both side gives,

$$\ln R(t) = -gt^m. \tag{2}$$

Multiplying through by -1 and taking the ln of both sides gives

$$\ln[-\ln R(t)] = m \ln t + \ln g. \tag{3}$$

The unbiased estimate of the reliability function is given by

$$R(t_i) = (N+1-i)/(N+1). \tag{4}$$

Because

$$-\ln[(N+1-i)/(N+1)] = \ln[(N+1)/N+1-i)], \tag{5}$$

equations 4 and 5 can be substituted into equation 3, providing

the following equation:

$$\ln \ln[(N+1)/(N+1-i)] = m \ln t + \ln g. \tag{6}$$

This is in the form

$$y = mx + b, \tag{7}$$

if the ordinate has an ln-ln scale and the abscissa has a ln scale (Chatfield, 1983; Forgione, 1963). Indeed, Weibull probability paper is constructed so that the data represented in equation 6 can be plotted as a straight line. Combining equations 6 and 7,

$$y = \ln [\ln (N+1)/(N+1-i)] = mx + b = m[\ln (t)] + \ln (g).$$

Therefore,

$$y = \ln [\ln (N+1)/(N+1-i)];$$

$$x = \ln (t);$$

$$b = \ln (g);$$

$$m = \text{slope of the line of best fit.}$$

If $\ln [(N+1) / (N+1-i)]$ is plotted against t_i on log-log graph paper and if the Weibull model is appropriate, then the points will lie approximately on a straight line (Chatfield, 1983). The slope of the line-of-best fit can be determined on Weibull plot paper by drawing a parallel line onto the Weibull slope indicator, which is on the top left corner of the Weibull plot paper.

The value of g can be determined at the value of t where $\ln [(N+1)/(N+1-i)] = 1$.

The Weibull reliability function is given by $R(t) = \exp[-gt^m]$.

Thus, $\ln R(t) = -gt^m$,

$\ln [-\ln R(t)] = m \ln t + \ln g$,

$\ln [-\ln R(t)] - \ln g = m \ln t$,

ln [-ln (N+1-i)/(N+1)] – ln g = m ln t,

ln [ln (N+1)/(N+1-i)] – ln g = m ln t,

ln [1] – ln g = m ln t,

0 – ln g = m ln t,

m ln t = - ln g.

The first failure, in this example, occurred at 67 hours.

Thus, reduce the Weibull distribution to a two-parameter

distribution by adjusting the location parameter:

m ln (t - 67) = - ln g.

Remember, the Weibull distribution has three

parameters: the scale parameter, the shape parameter, and

the location parameter (King, 1971). In short, the Weibull

distribution can be affectively reduced to a two-parameter

distribution by adjusting the location parameter. This will

help linearize the Weibull line and improve the ability to

estimate parameters. Using actual failure times from

Table 4, this is done by subtracting the time to first failure

from all failure times such that the first failure occurs at a

time equal to zero (Chatfield, 1983; Mann, Schafer, &

Singpurwalla, 1974). This effectively reduces the sample

size to $N = 9$ failed items, with the time to failure being

the $(i\text{-}1)$th failure after the smallest failure time, 67 hours.

Therefore, the $\ln [(N+1) / (N+1 - (i\text{-}1))]$ will be plotted

against t_i on log-log graph paper. Table 15 shows the

tabulated results.

Table 15

Checking if the Weibull Model is Appropriate for a Given Set of Data. $\ln \dfrac{(N+1)}{N+1-(i-1)} = \ln \dfrac{10}{(11-i)}.$ Using N = 9.

ITEM i	LIFE HOURS t_i	ADJUSTED LIFE HOURS $t_i - 67$	$\dfrac{(N+1)}{N+1-(i-1)}$	$\ln \dfrac{(N+1)}{N+1-(i-1)}$
1	67	0		
2	124	57	10/(11-2) = 1.11	ln 1.11 = .105
3	161	94	10/(11-3) = 1.25	ln 1.25 = .223
4	185	118	10/(11-4) = 1.43	ln 1.43 = .358
5	217	150	10/(11-5) = 1.67	ln 1.67 = .513
6	225	158	10/(11-6) = 2.0	ln 2.0 = .693
7	261	194	10/(11-7) = 2.5	ln 2.5 = .916
8	297	230	10/(11-8) = 3.33	ln 3.33 = 1.20
9	342	275	10/(11-9) = 5.0	ln 5.0 = 1.61
10	428	361	10/(11-10) = 10.0	ln 10.0 = 2.30

From Table 15, the adjusted life hours are plotted against the ln [(N + 1) / (N + 1 - (i - 1))] values. The plot is indicated in Figure 25. The result is a straight line, indicating that the Weibull distribution is appropriate to describe the tested data.

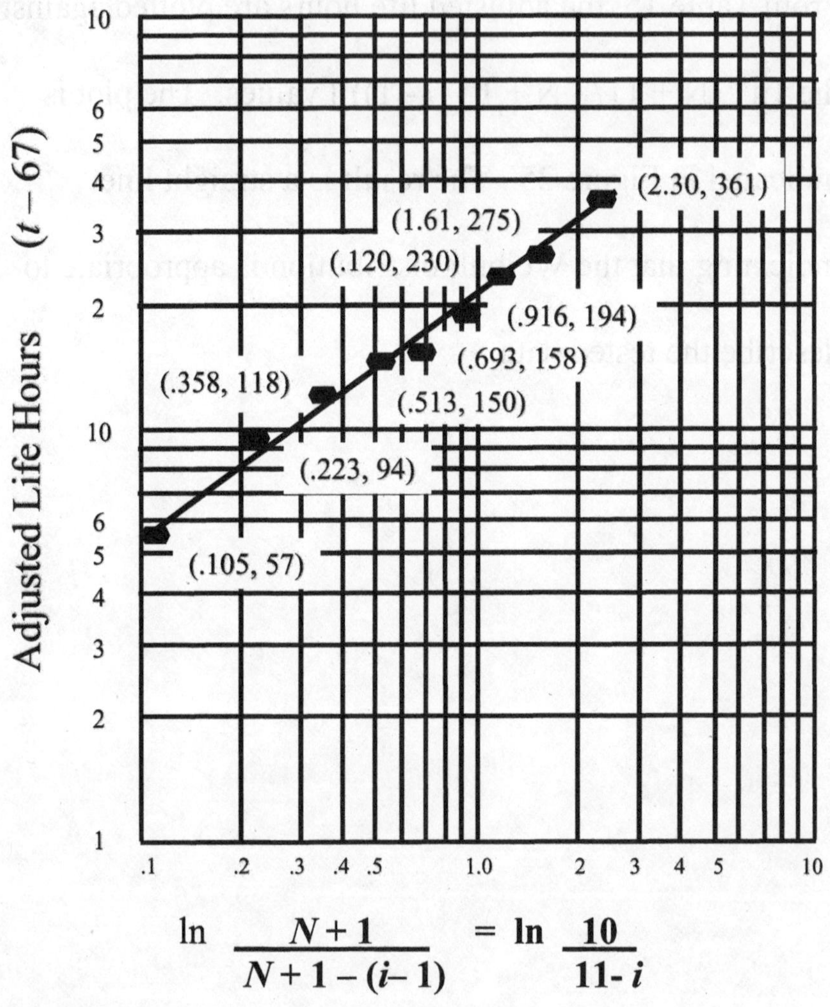

$$\ln \frac{N+1}{N+1-(i-1)} = \ln \frac{10}{11-i}$$

Figure 25. Checking if the Weibull Model is Appropriate for a Given Set of Data.

108

In conclusion, the Weibull distribution analysis can be quite useful for providing reliability assessment data on very small sample sizes. The analysis provides important information about the nature of failure. In short, the Weibull plot can describe a product's distribution shape, failure rate, and life that a given percent are expected to fail. It can also describe the confidence interval for the true life that a given percent are expected to fail and the confidence interval for the true percent failing at a given life (Ford Motor Company, 1968).

CHAPTER 3

Enhancing Reliability by Using Normal Probability Paper

Figure 26. Manipulating the manufacturing process to control the average size and variance of machined pieces during a production run.

This chapter describes how to assess the reliability of a manufacturing process when specifications, such as dimensions, must be satisfied. Product reliability can be improved if control over the manufacturing process is maintained. Once data values on the finished product are plotted, and if the data are normally distributed, then normal probability plots can be used to resolve out-of-specification conditions (Ford Motor Company, 1972). Graphical representations of the average and variance can be used to demonstrate how to minimize scrap, which will reduce cost. In other words, greater reliability over the manufacturing process will result in less scrap (i.e., greater reliability over the manufacturing process will result in consistently producing a good product).

Problems that will be addressed

in this Chapter

All problems and solutions in this chapter are based

on a ± 3 standard deviation manufacturing capability,

which cover 99.7% of the machined pieces. Therefore, a

statement that refers to the elimination of all scrap parts

means the elimination of all scrap parts within the ± 3

standard deviation manufacturing capability. In other

words, it is the best condition that can be achieved with

the current manufacturing process. It is acknowledged

that 0.3% of the pieces will fall outside the analysis

(100% - 99.7% = 0.3%).

The line-of-best fit will describe the data from - 3

standard deviations to + 3 standard deviations. In other

words, the line-of-best fit will extend from one side of the

distribution curve to the other side of the distribution

curve such that it describes 99.7% of the data. However,

the goal is to get 99.7% of the data to fall between the

lower and upper specification standards. Because the

line-of-best fit is defined by the mean and variance, the

mean and variance can be manipulated to achieve the

goal. In the following examples, the specification

standards, mean, and variance are based on the size of the

machined pieces.

Problems

1) Given a ± 3 standard deviation manufacturing capability, and given the upper and lower specification standards, determine the maximum value for one standard deviation that will allow for the elimination of all scrap parts.

2) By changing only the average part size, determine the change in the average part size that will eliminate all parts smaller than the lower specification standard.

3) By changing only the average part size, minimize the total number of out-of-specification parts within ± 3 standard deviations from the mean.

4) Enhancing the solution from Problem 3, change the variance in order to eliminate all out-of-specification parts within ± 3 standard deviations from the mean.

Mean and Standard Deviation

The mean is the average of the numbers, which is a calculated central value of the data set (Moore, 2000). The standard deviation, which is the square root of the variance, is a measure of how spread out the numbers are about the mean. For the following examples, ± 3 standard deviations will be used as the manufacturing capability. This ± 3 standard deviations benchmark will include 99.7% of the pieces manufactured during a production run.

Normal Density Curve

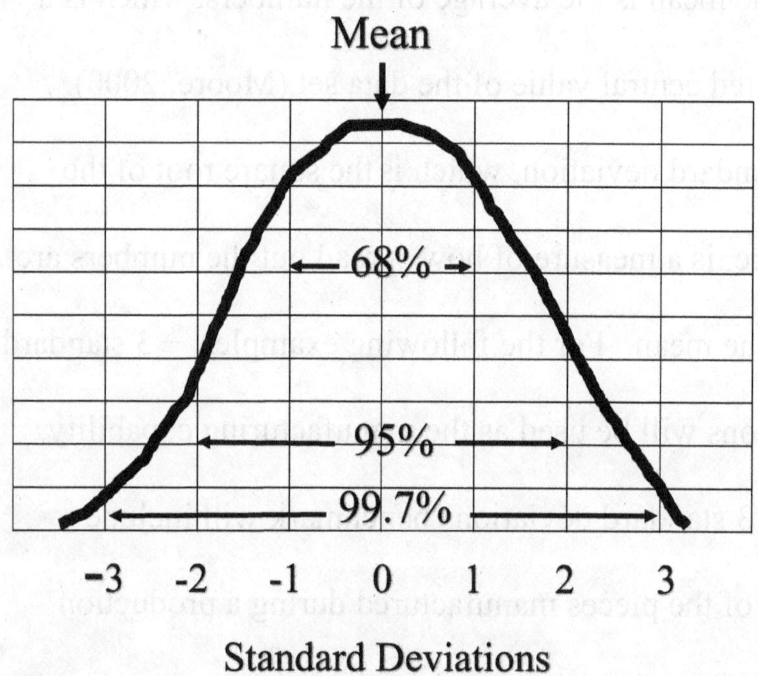

Figure 27. Normal density curve and standard deviations.

For the following examples, the data will reflect a normal distribution (i.e., a bell curve). Therefore, normal probability paper will be used to assess the data. Normal probability paper is a useful tool for learning how to effectively manipulate the mean and variance of the data so that the data will fall within specific standards (Ford Motor Company, 1972). In short, the average and the variance of the data can be described by a line-of-best fit. Therefore, manipulating the line-of-best fit to meet the goal will indicate the changes that are required for the average and variance to meet the goal.

The average and variance of a machined part can be manipulated via the manufacturing process (Ford Motor Company, 1972). For example, changing a product's average size between the lower specification and upper

specification can be achieved by changing the tool setup.

In addition, changing a product's variance can be

achieved by manipulating the machining speed, fixtures,

and locating pads.

Shifting the Mean to Eliminate Scrap

When using machines on the assembly line to create

widgets, there will be some variation in the final product's

dimensions due to limited resources, limited technology,

and changes in the environment (Ford Motor Company,

1972). For example, the tool setup and fixtures may

change, tools and locating pads may wear down,

machining speeds may not be effectively regulated, and

temperatures may change. Some of these variables, such as fixtures and machining speeds, can be manipulated to reduce product variance. Reducing product variance will improve product consistency and minimize waste.

A normal distribution is described by its average and standard deviation. Thus, by manipulating the average and standard deviation, the number of scrap parts can be reduced. For the following examples, assume that there is a ± 3 standard deviation manufacturing capability. By using normal probability paper, the solutions can be worked out graphically.

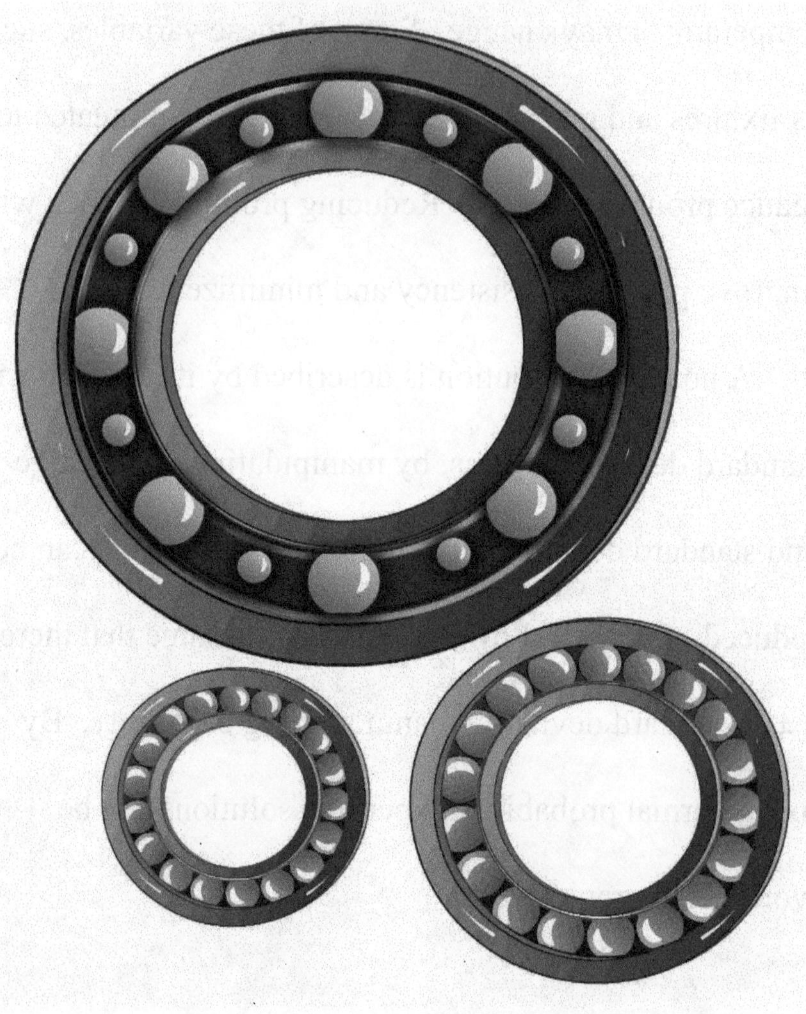

Figure 28. Widgets to be manufactured.

For this chapter, 3 standard deviations above the mean and 3 standard deviations below the mean will be considered within manufacturing capability. In addition, only the parts that fall between the lower specification standard and upper specification standard will be considered acceptable. The parts that are bigger than the upper standard or smaller than the lower standard will be considered scrap. See Figure 29 for data that will be used to solve problems 1 - 4.

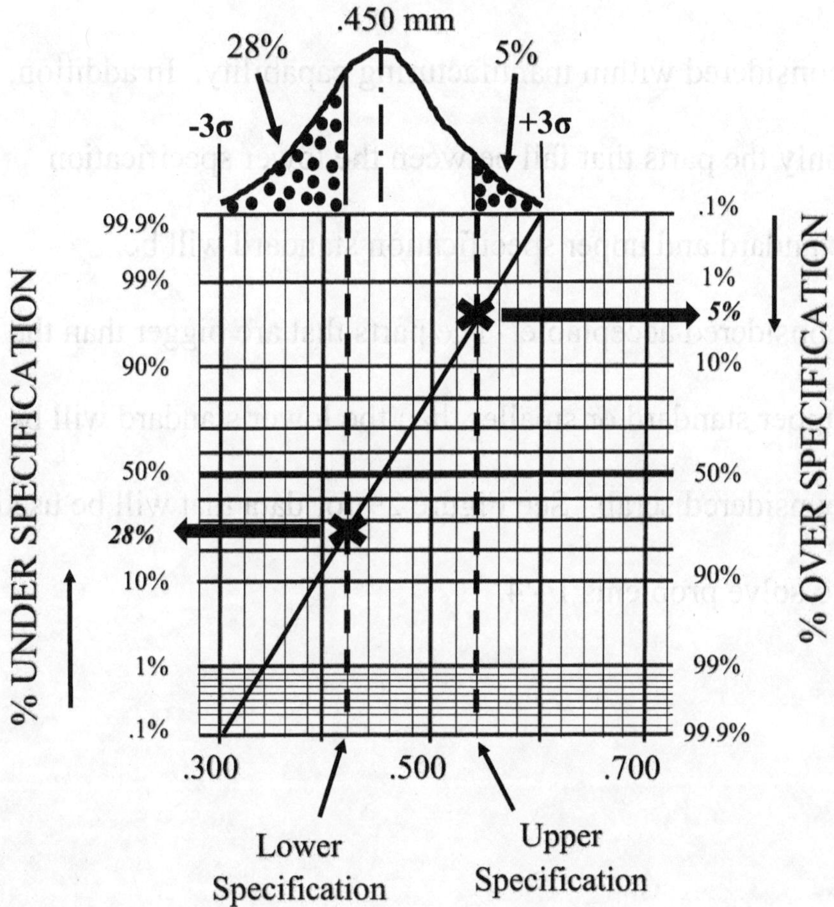

Figure 29. Original setup with 28% of the parts below specification and 5% above specification. X-axis scale = mm.

<u>**Problem 1**</u>

Given a ± 3 standard deviation manufacturing capability, and given the upper and lower specification standards, determine the maximum value for one standard deviation that will allow for the elimination of all scrap parts.

Solution for Problem 1

Upper Specification = 0.540 mm;

Lower Specification = 0.420 mm.

Sigma = σ = one standard deviation

Total sigma (σ) capability = **± 3σ**

± 3σ = 6σ capability, which includes 99.7% of the

pieces during a production run.

In order to eliminate all scrap, the + 3σ must be set equal

to the upper specification and the - 3σ must be set equal to

the lower specification such that 99.7% of the parts are

contained between the upper and lower specifications. In

other words, the 6σ capability = Upper Specification –

Lower Specification.

Therefore, to solve the problem,

6σ capability = Upper Specification – Lower Specification;

$$\sigma = \frac{\text{Upper Specification} - \text{Lower Specification}}{6} \ ;$$

$$\sigma = \frac{0.540 \text{ mm} - 0.420 \text{ mm}}{6} = \frac{0.120 \text{ mm}}{6} = 0.020 \text{ mm}.$$

Thus, if the Upper Specification = .540 mm and the

Lower Specification = .420 mm, then the number of scrap

parts will be minimized if the maximum value for σ (one

standard deviation) = 0.020 mm.

Interpreting Normal Probability Paper

As stated earlier, several factors can affect a
machined product's average size and variance. For
example, the tool setup can affect the product's average
size (Ford Motor Company, 1972). In addition, the
machining speed, locating pads, and fixtures can impact
the product's variance. Thus, because the average and
variation can be manipulated, the number of out-of-
specification pieces can be effectively managed.

The following exercises will manipulate graphical
representations on normal probability paper in order to
shed light on how to improve product reliability. The
goal is to enhance the reliability of the manufacturing
process in order to make consistent parts and to reduce the

number of scrap parts. Reducing the number of scrap

parts will reduce cost.

Problem 2

By changing only the average part size,

determine the change in the average part size

that will eliminate all parts smaller than the

lower specification standard.

Given: Use Data on Figure 29.

Upper Specification = 0.540 mm;

Lower Specification = 0.420 mm;

Mean = 0.450 mm.

Based on Figure 29, with the current manufacturing process, 28% of the parts are below specification (intersection between line-of-best fit and the lower specification line) and 5% are above specification (intersection between line-of-best fit and the upper specification line)

(• = out of specification).

Objective: Eliminate the 28% parts below specification without changing the standard deviation.

The standard deviation is determined by the slope of the line-of-best fit and will not be changed by shifting the original line-of-best fit in a parallel fashion. Therefore, shift the line-of-best fit in a parallel fashion so that the parts smaller than the lower specification are eliminated. See Figure 30. In the field, this can be accomplished by changing the tool setup, which affects the average part size. Increasing the average part size, which is indicated by the peak on the normal distribution curve, will shift the distribution curve to the right.

Graphically, eliminating the parts smaller than the lower specification standard is accomplished by intersecting the line-of-best fit with the lower most horizontal line of the lower specification. Effectively, the

- 3σ value has been aligned to the lower specification

standard, which will eliminate all parts to the left of the

lower specification standard.

However, notice in Figure 30 that the percentage of

parts bigger than the upper specification standard has now

increased from 5% to 70% (intersection between the line-

of-best fit and the upper specification line). Thus,

although the number of parts smaller than the lower

specification standard has been eliminated, the number of

parts bigger than the upper specification standard has

increased. The problem has gotten worse (the original

33% total out-of-specification has increased to 70% total

out-of-specification).

Notice in Figure 30 that the bell curve shifted to the right by 0.120 mm (from .450 mm to .570 mm). This means that the average size for the part has increased by 0.120 mm (from .450 mm to .570 mm). As indicated by the slope of the line-of-best fit, the variance of the data did not change.

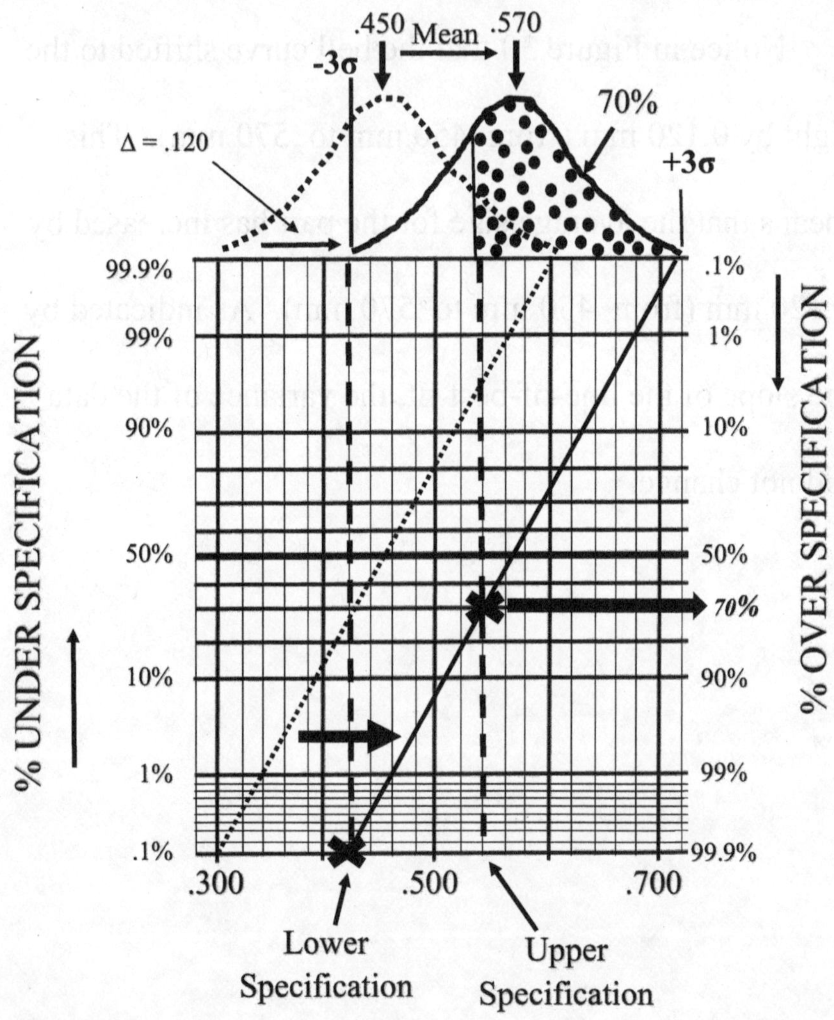

Figure 30. Elimination of scrap parts below lower specification. However, the percentage of scrap parts above specification has now increased (• = out of specification). X-axis scale = mm.

Problem 3

By changing only the average part size, minimize

the total number of out-of-specification parts

within ± 3 standard deviations from the mean.

Given: Use Data on Figure 29.

Upper Specification = 0.540 mm;

Lower Specification = 0.420 mm;

Mean = 0.450 mm.

<u>**Solution to Problem 3**</u>

Although simply shifting the line-of-best fit (parallel shift with no slope change) allowed the elimination of scrap parts below the lower specification standard, it increased the number of scrap parts above the upper specification standard. In order to minimize the total number of scrap parts above and below the specification standards, and without changing the variance, the distribution curve and the line-of-best fit must both be centered between the lower and upper specification standards. First, using the data given in Figure 29, shift the distribution curve so that its mean aligns with the midpoint between the specification standards. The midpoint between the lower and upper specification

standards = 0.420 + (0.540 – 0.420) / 2 = 0.420 + 0.06 =

0.480.   Thus, by centering the mean of the distribution

curve between the lower and upper specification

standards, the mean has increased from 0.450 mm to .480

mm. See Figure 31. This shift maximizes the amount of

the distribution curve within the range of the specification

standards. Second, after the distribution curve has been

shifted, shift the line-of-best fit in a parallel fashion so

that it intersects the 50% line and mean value of the

distribution curve (.480 mm).

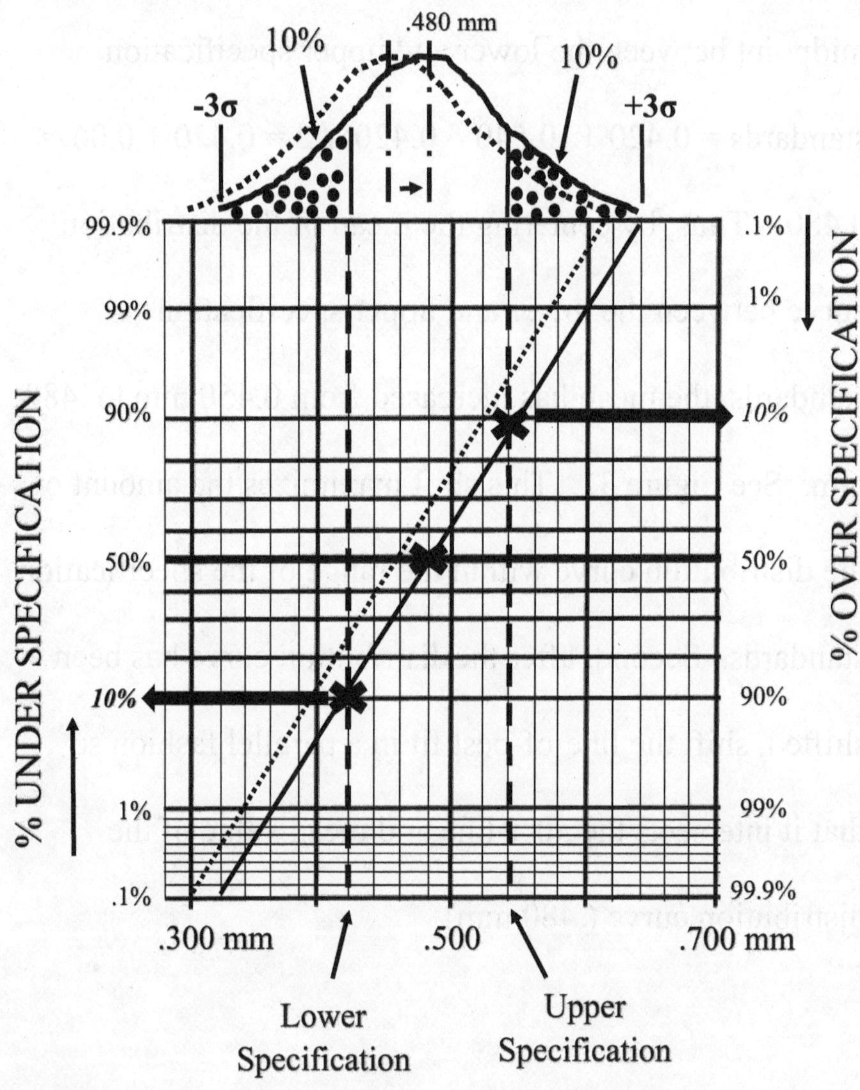

Figure 31. Minimizing the total number of scrap parts without modifying the variation (• = out of specification).

136

In Figure 31, the distribution curve has been shifted to the right and centered between the lower and upper specifications. The line-of-best fit has been shifted in a parallel fashion such that it crosses the 50% line at the mean value of the distribution curve. The line-of-best fit continues to cover the ± 3 standard deviations of the density curve.

According to Figure 31, the percentage of parts smaller than the lower specification standard is determined by the intersection of the line-of-best fit and the lower specification line, which is 10%. The percentage of parts bigger than the upper specification standard is determined by the intersection of the line-of-best fit and the upper specification line, which is 10%.

Thus, the total percent out-of-specification in this exercise

is 20%, which is the lowest possible without modifying

the variance. Indeed, most of the density curve has been

contained between the lower and upper specification

standards; only the extremes of the bell curve, which is a

very low percentage, fall out-of-specification. To verify

the solution, the 20% scrap (indicated in Figure 31) is

lower than the original 33% scrap (indicated in Figure

29).

In sum, the distribution of the data depends on the

manufacturing process. In order to enhance reliability

and to minimize scrap, the manufacturing process can be

manipulated. In practice, one way to accomplish this is

by changing the product's average size. In the field, the

product's average size can be manipulated by changing the tool setup. Another way to enhance reliability and to minimize scrap, as will be demonstrated in Problem 4, is to manipulate the product's variance.

Problem 4

Given: Continue with Data on Figure 31.

Enhancing the solution from Problem 3, change the variance in order to eliminate all out-of-specification parts within ± 3 standard deviations from the mean.

Solution to Problem 4

Start from Figure 31. Although minimizing the total

number of scrap parts without modifying the variation has

improved the situation, there is still 20% waste (10%

below specification and 10% above specification). In

order to eliminate all waste within ± 3 standard deviations

from the mean, the variance must also be manipulated.

This can be accomplished by adjusting the slope of the

line-of-best fit so that the line-of-best fit intersects the

upper most and lower most horizontal lines at the lower

and upper specifications. The solution is presented in

Figure 32.

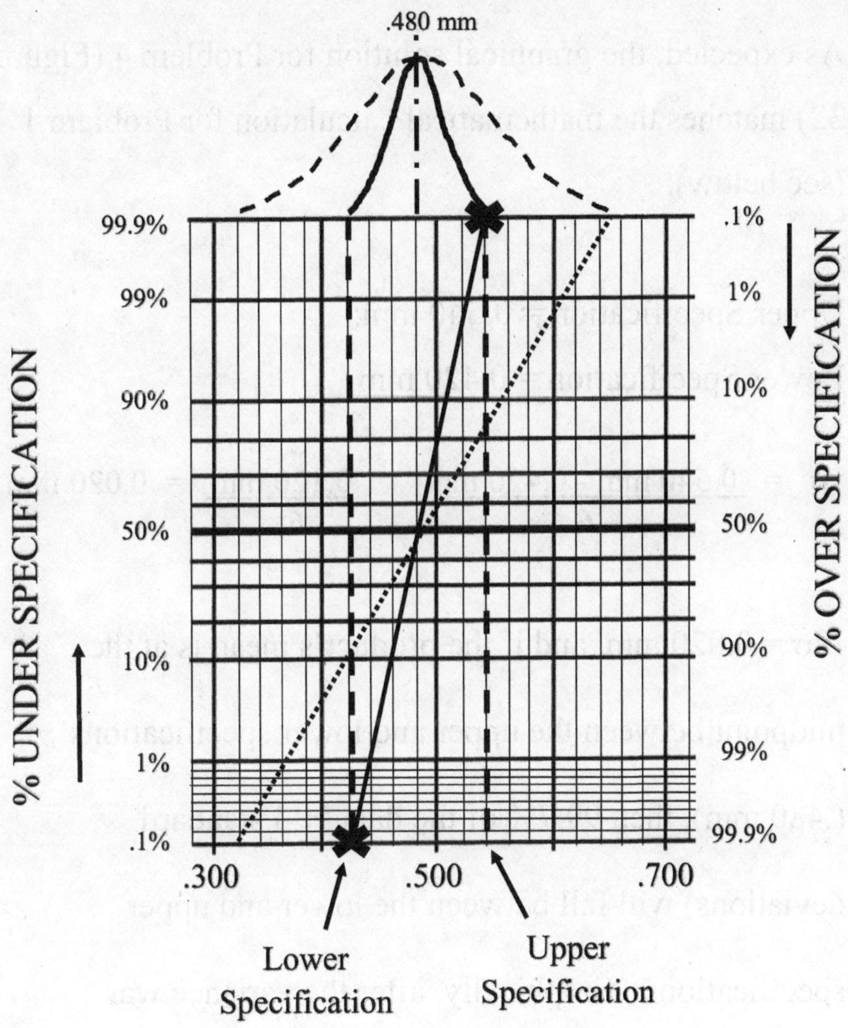

Figure 32. Eliminating the total number of scrap parts by also manipulating the variation. X-axis scale = mm.

As expected, the graphical solution for Problem 4 (Figure 32) matches the mathematical calculation for Problem 1 (see below).

Upper Specification = 0.540 mm;
Lower Specification = 0.420 mm.

$$\sigma = \frac{0.540 \text{ mm} - 0.420 \text{ mm}}{6} = \frac{0.120 \text{ mm}}{6} = 0.020 \text{ mm}$$

If $\sigma = 0.020$ mm, and if the product's mean is at the midpoint between the upper and lower specifications (.480 mm), then 99.7% of the data (± 3 standard deviations) will fall between the lower and upper specifications. Graphically, after the variance was changed, there are no parts to the left of the lower specification standard and no parts to the right of the upper specification standard. The line-of-best fit, which

extends from one side of the distribution curve to the

other side of the distribution curve, describes 99.7% of

the data. In short, the line-of-best fit extends from the

lower specification line to the upper specification line and

describes 99.7% of the data.

Summary

There are three sequential steps to take when utilizing normal probability plots to enhance reliability.

1) Center the peak of the distribution curve (i.e., the mean) between the upper and lower specification standards.

2) Center the line-of-best fit such that it crosses the 50% horizontal line at the mean value of the distribution curve.

3) Adjust the slope of the line-of-best fit so that the line-of-best fit intersects the upper most and lower most horizontal lines at the lower and upper specifications.

Practice Problem

Given: Use Data on Figure 33.

Reduce as much waste as possible within ± 3 standard deviations from the mean. There is a 6 sigma (σ) manufacturing capability. Determine the value of one standard deviation such that the number of scrap products are eliminated. The waste is currently at 43%.

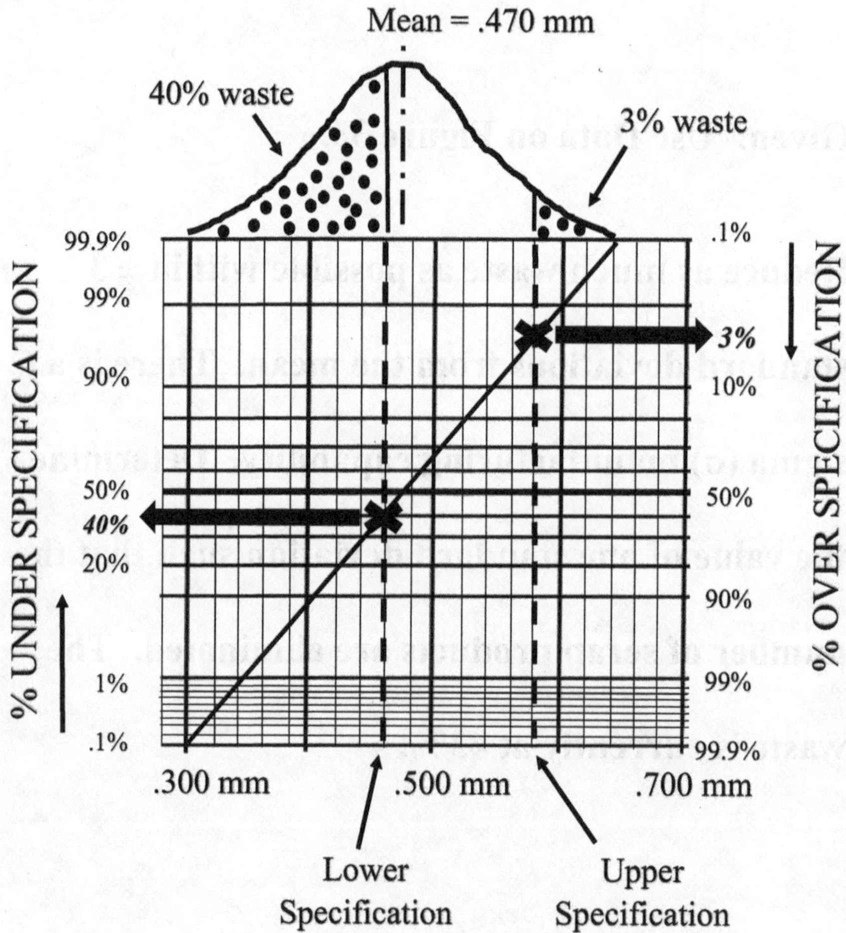

Figure 33. Practice Problem. The above information is given and the exercise is to reduce waste (• = out of specification).

<u>Solution to Practice Problem</u>

Step 1) Center the distribution curve between the upper and lower specification standards (this changes the average part size).

Step 2) Center the line-of-best fit, without changing its slope, such that it crosses the 50% horizontal line at the mean of the distribution curve (this provides the lowest possible number of scrap parts without modifying the variance).

Step 3) Adjust the slope of the line-of-best fit so that the line-of-best fit intersects the upper most and lower most horizontal lines at the lower and upper specification standards (this changes the variance and eliminates the number of scrap parts within the manufacturing capability).

Step 4) Use the 6 sigma manufacturing capability to
calculate the value of one standard deviation so
that the number of scrap parts will be eliminated
within the manufacturing capability.

<u>Solution to Practice Problem</u>

<u>Steps 1-2: Compare Figure 33 to Figure 34</u>

Step 1) Center the distribution curve between the upper and lower specification standards. The distribution curve in Figure 33 has been shifted to that in Figure 34. Centering the mean of the distribution curve between the specification standards changes the average part size from 0.470 mm to .520 mm.

Step 2) Without changing its slope, center the line-of-best fit such that it crosses the 50% horizontal line at the mean value of the distribution curve (50% at 0.520 mm). Notice the total scrap has been reduced from 43% to 30%. Figure 34 is the result of Steps 1 - 2.

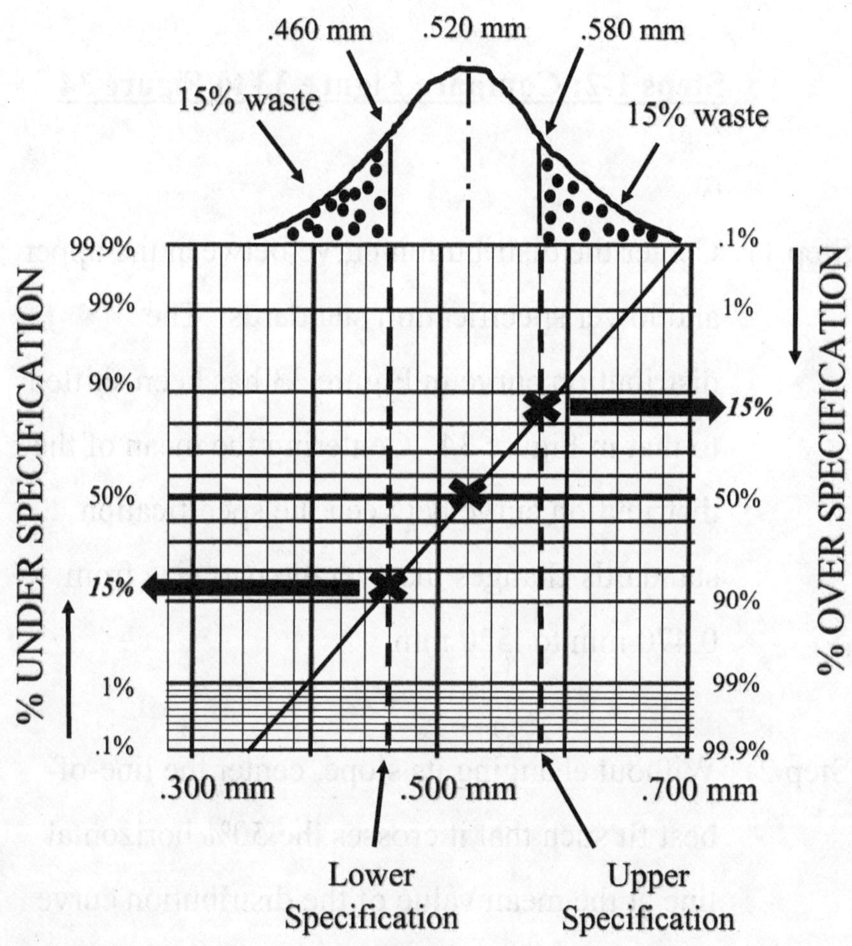

Figure 34. Reducing waste by only adjusting the average piece size. (• = out of specification)

150

<u>Step 3: Compare Figure 34 to Figure 35</u>

Step 3) Adjust the slope of the line-of-best fit (i.e., the variance) so that the line-of-best fit intersects the upper most and lower most horizontal lines at the lower and upper specification standards. This will eliminate all scrap parts within the manufacturing capability. Figure 35 is the final result of Steps 1 - 3.

<u>**Step 4 is Based on Figure 35**</u>

Step 4) Given the specification standards, if the mean is

0.520 mm, calculate the value of one standard

deviation so that all scrap parts will be eliminated

within the manufacturing capability.

There is a 6 sigma manufacturing capability

6 σ = (0.580 mm - 0.460 mm) = 0.120 mm

σ = (0.120 mm / 6) = 0.020 mm

Therefore, if the lower specification standard = 0.460

mm, if the upper specification standard = 0.580 mm,

if the mean part size = 0.520 mm, and if one standard

deviation $\leq$ 0.020 mm, then all scrap parts within

manufacturing capability will be eliminated. See Figure

35.

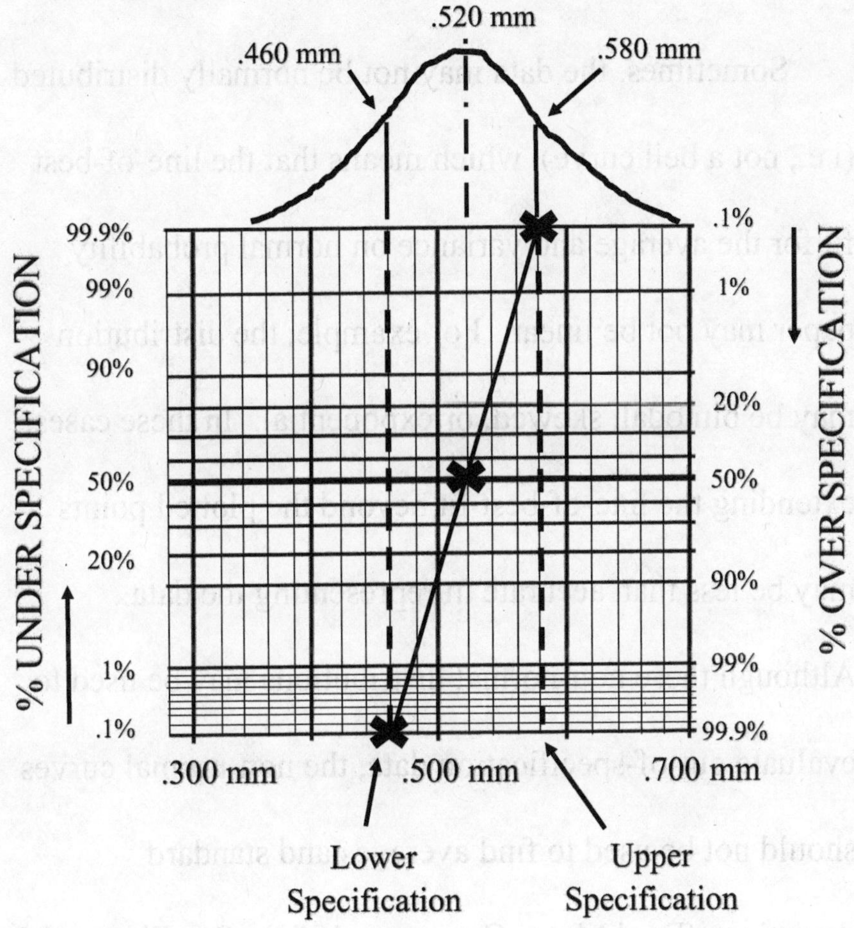

Figure 35. Reducing waste by adjusting the average piece size and by adjusting the variance of the machined pieces.

Final Note: Non-normal Distributions

Sometimes, the data may not be normally distributed

(i.e., not a bell curve), which means that the line-of-best

fit for the average and variance on normal probability

paper may not be linear. For example, the distribution

may be bimodal, skewed, or exponential. In these cases,

extending the line-of-best fit beyond the plotted points

may be less than accurate in representing the data.

Although these non-normal distributions may be used to

evaluate out-of-specification data, the non-normal curves

should not be used to find averages and standard

deviations (Ford Motor Company, 1972). See Figures 36

- 38 for graphical representations of these non-normal

distributions.

Bimodal Distribution

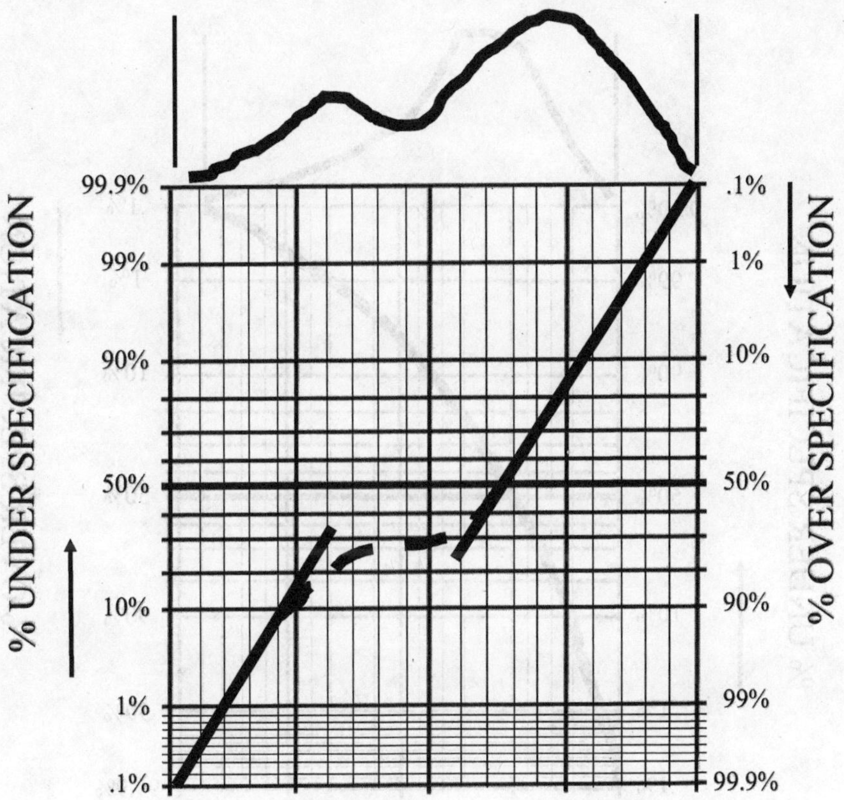

Figure 36. Non-normal distribution of data: Bimodal.

Skewed Distribution

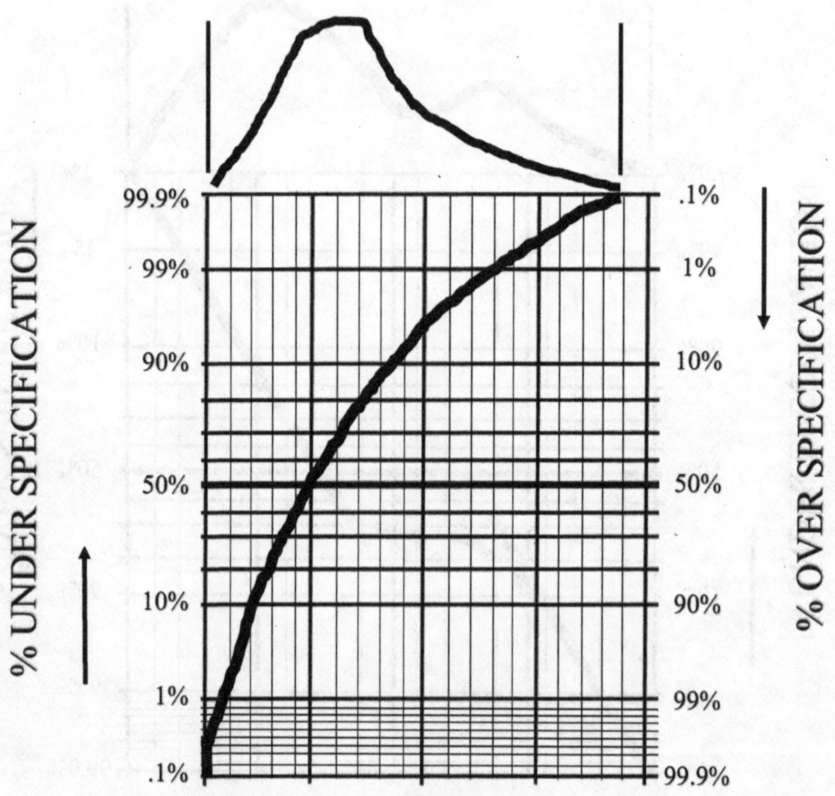

Figure 37. Non-normal distribution of data: Skewed.

Exponential Distribution

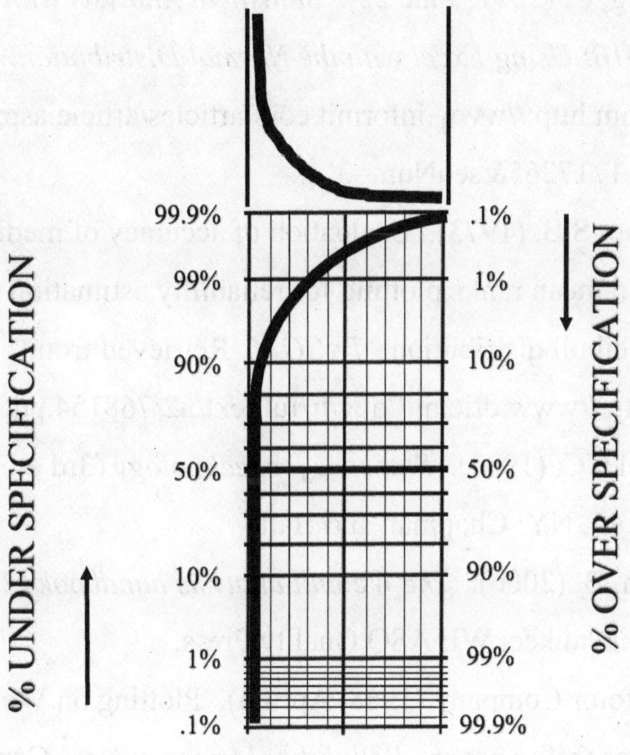

Figure 38. Non-normal distribution of data: Exponential.

References

Carlberg, C. (2011, June 22). *Statistical Analysis with Excel 2010: Using Excel with the Normal Distribution*. Retrieved from http://www.informit.com/articles/article.aspx? p=1717265&seqNum=3

Catalano, S.B. (1973). Evaluation of accuracy of median ranks and mean ranks plotting for reliability estimation using the Weibull distribution. *TACOM*. Retrieved from http://www.dtic.mil/dtic/tr/fulltext/u2/768154.pdf

Chatfield, C. (1983). *Statistics for technology* (3rd ed.). New York, NY: Chapman and Hall.

Dodson, B. (2006). *The Weibull analysis handbook* (2nd ed.). Milwaukee, WI: ASQ Quality Press.

Ford Motor Company (1968, April 4). Plotting on Weibull probability paper. *Reliability Memorandum*. General Parts Division.

Ford Motor Company (1969, November 21). Calculation of median rank values and the method of handling suspended items. *Reliability Memorandum*. General Parts Division.

Ford Motor Company (1972, January). *Reliability methods: Interpreting normal probability paper – Module III.* Reliability Office, North American Automotive Operations.

Forgione, J. (1963, April 26). Weibull-Johnson statistical analysis of failure data. *Reliability Reference Manual - Methods Paper 1.* Ford Motor Company Reliability Engineering Group.

Grant, E.L., & Leavenworth, R.S. (1980). *Statistical quality control* (5th ed.). New York, NY: McGraw-Hill.

Kapur, K.C. & Lamberson, L.R. (1977). *Reliability in engineering design.* New York, N: Wiley.

King, J.R. (1971). *Probability charts for decision making.* New York, NY: Industrial Press.

Lyer, R.K. (2013). ECE 313 Probability with Engineering Applications Lecture 20. Retrieved from https://courses.engr.illinois.edu/ece313/fa2013/SectionB/Lectures/lec_20.pdf

Mann, N.R., Schafer, R.E., Singpurwalla, N.D. (1974). *Methods for statistical analysis of reliability and life data.* New York, NY: Wiley.

Marshall, J. (2012). *An Introduction to Reliability and Life Distributions*. The University of Warwick. Retrieved from http://www2.warwick.ac.uk/fac/sci/wmg/ftmsc/modules/ modulelist/peuss/slides/section_8b_peussdistributions_2_sl ides_compatibility_mode.pdf

MathPages (n.d.). *Weibull Analysis*. Retrieved from http://www.mathpages.com/home/kmath122/kmath122.htm

McLinn, J.A. (1988, September). Product reliability: Extending quality's reach. *Manufacturing Engineering*, 52-55.

Moore, D.S. (2000). *The basic practice of statistics* (2nd ed.). New York, NY: Freeman and Company.

Weibull.com (2001, October). Probability plotting. *Reliability Engineering Resource*. Retrieved from http://weibull.com/hotwire/issue8/relbasics8.htm

Weibull.com (2002, April). Characteristics of the Weibull distribution. *Reliability Engineering Resource*. Retrieved from http://www.weibull.com/hotwire/issue14/ relbasics14.htm

Weibull.com (2002, May). Location parameter of the Weibull distribution. *Reliability Engineering Resource*. Retrieved

from http://www.weibull.com/hotwire/issue15/relbasics
15.htm